GREAT LIVES OBSERVED

Gerald Emanuel Stearn, *General Editor*

EACH VOLUME IN THE SERIES VIEWS THE CHARACTER AND
ACHIEVEMENT OF A GREAT WORLD FIGURE IN THREE PER-
SPECTIVES—THROUGH HIS OWN WORDS, THROUGH THE OPIN-
IONS OF HIS CONTEMPORARIES, AND THROUGH RETROSPECTIVE
JUDGMENTS—THUS COMBINING THE INTIMACY OF AUTOBIOG-
RAPHY, THE IMMEDIACY OF EYEWITNESS OBSERVATION, AND
THE OBJECTIVITY OF MODERN SCHOLARSHIP.

WILLIAM M. TUTTLE, JR., editor of this volume in the Great
Lives Observed series, is a member of the history department
at the University of Kansas. The author of the award-winning
Race Riot: Chicago in the Red Summer of 1919, Tuttle has
also published articles in the *Journal of American History, Labor History, Journal of Negro History, Phylon*, and *American
Studies*. In addition, he has been a Senior Fellow in Southern
and Negro History at Johns Hopkins University, a Younger
Humanist Fellow of the National Endowment for the Human-
ities, and a Research Fellow at the Charles Warren Center,
Harvard University.

Acknowledgments

Many people have assisted me in the writing and editing of this volume. I want particularly to thank David M. Katzman, the University of Kansas; Paul G. Partington of Whittier, California; Charles Cooney of the Manuscript Division, Library of Congress; Robert C. Twombly, the City College of New York; and the staffs of the Library of Congress; the Houghton and Widener Libraries, Harvard University; Watson Library, University of Kansas; and the Schomburg Collection of Negro Literature and History, New York Public Library. I am also very much indebted to Heide Gold, of Harvard University's Charles Warren Center for Studies in American History, who typed the manuscript, and to Sarah Minden Faux, of Brandeis University, who helped me to read and correct the galley proofs.

Many individuals and editors of journals have graciously granted me permission to reprint various writings. For such permissions, I am grateful to Henry Lee Moon of *The Crisis;* the Crisis Publishing Company; the National Association for the Advancement of Colored People; Winston R. Coleman, *The Quarterly Review of Higher Education among Negroes;* Marie B. Frazier; Amy Jacques-Garvey; Esther Jackson, *Freedomways;* Hyman Lumer, *Political Affairs;* August Meier and The University of Michigan Press; A. Philip Randolph; and Morris B. Rubin, *The Progressive.*

Finally, I should like to dedicate this book to my children. Hopefully, they will grow to understand what W. E. B. Du Bois spent a lifetime trying to teach: That one need not—and indeed should not —renounce one's heritage or deny one's identity in order to hope for and pursue first-class citizenship. The black man or woman, Du Bois wrote in 1897 "simply wishes to make it possible for a man [or a woman] to be both a Negro and an American without being cursed and spit upon . . . [and] without losing the opportunity of self-development." When and if this ideal becomes a reality, the United States will have taken a crucial step toward fulfilling its promise to the world.   WILLIAM M. TUTTLE, JR.

GREAT LIVES OBSERVED

W.E.B. Du Bois

Edited by William M. Tuttle, Jr.

*One ever feels his
two-ness,—an American, a
Negro; two souls, two
thoughts, two unreconciled
strivings; two warring ideals
in one dark body, whose dogged
strength alone keeps it from
being torn asunder.*

W. E. B. Du Bois (1897)

A SPECTRUM BOOK

PRENTICE-HALL, INC., ENGLEWOOD CLIFFS, N.J.

Library of Congress Cataloging in Publication Data

TUTTLE, WILLIAM M comp.
    W. E. B. Du Bois.
    (Great lives observed) (A Spectrum Book)
    Bibliography: p.
    1. Du Bois, William Edward Burghardt, 1868–1963.
2. United States—Race question. 3. Negroes—Race
identity.
E185.97.D73T86 1973   301.24′2′0924 [B]   73–9544
ISBN 0–13–220905–5
ISBN 0–13–220889–X (pbk.)

To Bill, Kate, and Andrew

© 1973 by PRENTICE-HALL, INC.,
Englewood Cliffs, N.J.

A SPECTRUM BOOK

10 9 8 7 6 5 4 3 2 1

Printed in the United States of America

PRENTICE-HALL INTERNATIONAL, INC. (*London*)
PRENTICE-HALL OF AUSTRALIA PTY., LTD. (*Sydney*)
PRENTICE-HALL OF CANADA, LTD. (*Toronto*)
PRENTICE-HALL OF INDIA PRIVATE LIMITED (*New Delhi*)
PRENTICE-HALL OF JAPAN, INC. (*Tokyo*)

Contents

PART ONE

W. E. B. DU BOIS LOOKS AT BLACK AMERICA AND THE WORLD

1

2

3

4

5

6

Introduction

In the early 1960's, several thousand radical students on campuses in the United States established chapters of the W. E. B. Du Bois Club. Disillusioned with America and dismayed by the Cuban missile crisis, the country's deepening involvement in Southeast Asia, and the limited gains of the civil rights movement, these students sought revolutionary change. In so doing, they honored a man who had been in the forefront of the fight against racism and imperialism for over sixty years. Almost immediately the government of the United States, through its spokesmen in the Department of Justice and the Federal Bureau of Investigation, labeled the Du Bois Club an organization sponsored and directed by Communists, thereby seeking to discredit it.

Private citizens, some of them with political ambitions of their own, joined in denouncing these student activists, and in the process they revealed their ignorance of recent American history. One of these critics was Richard M. Nixon, a man whose political star seemed to have been permanently eclipsed by his defeats in 1960 for the presidency and in 1962 for the governorship of California. What particularly disturbed Mr. Nixon was the similarity in pronunciation between the names of the Du Bois Club and the Boys Clubs of America, of which he was the national board chairman. Decrying this similarity, in early 1966 he charged that it misled people into mistaking one organization for the other, adding that this confusion was "an almost classic case of Communist deception and duplicity." The Du Bois Clubs, he said, "are not unaware of the confusion they are causing among our supporters and among many other good citizens." If Mr. Nixon's accusation had not been so ludicrous, it could have been dangerous. One man, Theodore Hochstadt, writing to *The New York Times*, had sufficient good humor to comment on Mr. Nixon's claim. "In bringing to our attention the duplicity of the Du Bois Clubs in pronouncing their name 'Doo Boys,'" Hochstadt wrote, "Richard Nixon neglected to point out the extreme duplicity of W. E. B. Du Bois, who for many decades pronounced his name 'Doo Boys' as part of a long-range plot by which a subversive organization would be formed after his death

1

and would use his name because it could be easily confused with
the Boys Clubs." Hochstadt also congratulated Mr. Nixon on his
perspicacity in noting "the possibility that some of the 2,500 members of the Du Bois Clubs may be under the mistaken notion that
they are members of the Boys Clubs. . . ." But this was not necessarily a disaster, for "perhaps everything will even out, in terms of
misplaced members."

But if W. E. B. Du Bois was not the front man for an elaborate
Communist plot, who was he? To many people he was a hero and
a prophet. To Dr. Martin Luther King, Jr., Du Bois was "an intellectual giant" and a teacher. Speaking in 1968, in his last major
address before he was assassinated, King declared:

> One idea he [Du Bois] insistently taught was that black people have
> been kept in oppression and deprivation by a poisonous fog of lies
> that depicted them as inferior, born deficient and deservedly doomed
> to servitude to the grave. . . . So long as the lie was believed, the
> brutality and criminality of conduct toward the Negro was easy for
> the conscience to bear. . . . Dr. Du Bois recognized that the key-
> stone in the arch of oppression was the myth of inferiority and he
> dedicated his brilliant talents to demolish it.

To another black leader, Kwame Nkrumah, first president of newly
independent Ghana, Du Bois' greatness transcended the geographi-
cal limits of the United States. Nkrumah praised Du Bois for being
a "great African patriot" and "an undaunted fighter for the emancipation of colonial and oppressed people. . . ."

To others, both white and black, Du Bois was an evil man who
should be either jailed, ostracized, or deported. Speaking on the
floor of the United States House of Representatives in 1919, segrega-
tionist congressman James F. Byrnes of South Carolina accused
Du Bois of being a seditionary if not a traitor. "No greater service
can be rendered to the negro to-day," Byrnes declared, "than to have
him know that this Government will not tolerate on the part of a
leader of his race action which tends to array the negro race against
the Government under which they live and under which the race
has made greater strides than it has under any other Government on
earth. [Applause.]" Numerous blacks, among them the black nationalist Marcus Garvey of the Universal Negro Improvement Association, were also critical of Du Bois. Garvey, at one point, dismissed
Du Bois as "purely and simply a white man's nigger." And in 1934,
after Du Bois had resigned as editor of *The Crisis,* journal of the

National Association for the Advancement of Colored People,
Arthur C. Macneal, president of the NAACP's Chicago branch,
branded Du Bois a traitor to his race who was not only "more de-
testable than Benedict Arnold," but who should be "properly rele-
gated to the same fate if a worse one cannot be made. . . ."

W. E. B. Du Bois was controversial but, both occupationally and
ideologically, he was many other things as well—sociologist, historian, teacher, novelist, poet, editor, propagandist, civil rights activist, black nationalist, Pan-Africanist, anticolonialist, Marxist, and
political radical. Even for a man who lived to be ninety-five years
old, his interests and accomplishments were legion. For example, he
began his writing career as a teen-age newspaper correspondent in
the 1880's, and he continued to produce lucid prose until his death
in 1963. Yet in his writings and actions he seemed at times, and in
very basic ways, to contradict himself. How, some historians have
asked, could a civil rights leader, with an implicit commitment to
integration and the "American dream," also be a black nationalist,
even a black chauvinist? Writing in the late 1950's, Elliott Rudwick,
one of Du Bois' biographers, criticized him for this seeming incon-
sistency.[1] Du Bois, he wrote,

> desired not only self-segregation, but also insisted that his people
> should be allowed to participate fully in the common political,
> spiritual, and social life of the nation. But these dual goals were
> contradictory. . . . A highly disciplined . . . Negro social and eco-
> nomic system would have preserved in the minds of both races a
> sense of detached destinies and fostered among the colored people a
> glorification of separateness, thereby making it impossible for them
> to achieve full participation in the larger society.

As Francis Broderick, another of Du Bois' biographers, has commented upon these apparent contradictions. "Writing month after
month on current events, he [Du Bois] did not, of course, abruptly
end one period of intellectual change and begin another. He might
drop a hint, then wait twenty years before picking it up for further
development." In the opening years of the twentieth century, for
example, when he was one of the nation's leading black proponents
of agitation and protest for first-class citizenship for Afro-Americans,
Du Bois was also an advocate of "self-sufficient, segregated Negro
communities." In politics, too, Du Bois urged blacks to become the

[1] See Bibliographical Note for a discussion of books and articles by and about
Du Bois.

"balance of power" by voting as a bloc, seemingly overlooking, as Broderick points out, "the possibility that such a political device might not compel white justice, but might invite the alternative of removing the Negro from politics entirely." Moreover, in 1907 and 1908, at the same time that he "was making approaches to socialism . . . , he affirmed his attachment to the principles of the Republican party," and in 1912 he endorsed the Democratic candidate, Woodrow Wilson, for the presidency. Broderick has also observed that in the 1920's, while the goal of a biracial alliance of workers was uppermost in Du Bois' thought, "a minor theme, self-sufficiency for the Negro community, was rising in a crescendo which by the 1930's would make it dominant. . . . Conversely, as new ideas came to prominence after the World War, the old ones did not disappear. . . ." As noted earlier, Du Bois in 1934 resigned from his editorial and research post at the NAACP, in protest over its neglect of the economic bases of second-class citizenship; in 1944, however, he returned to work for the organization, even though most of its programs were no more in conformance with his ideas than they had been a decade earlier. And in 1961, Du Bois made application for membership in the Communist Party of the United States, an organization of which he had been an outspoken critic in the 1930's. "His ideas," Broderick has concluded, "changed constantly, but the major changes came gradually, with a considerable overlap."

Du Bois was a "paradox," as August Meier, another Du Bois scholar, has stated. Yet the United States and the world had been transformed dramatically during his lifetime, and many of his philosophical and ideological changes, modifications, and variations were responses to that new reality. Although at different times he endorsed different routes to liberation—whether it was liberation from American racism, from economic servitude, or from colonial bondage—his basic commitment remained constant: to equality of opportunity for attaining self-realization, human dignity, and a decent living without regard to race. As one might expect, Du Bois himself best expressed this commitment. "I believe," he wrote in 1920, "that all men, black and brown and white, are brothers, varying through Time and Opportunity, in form and gift and feature, but differing in no essential particular, and alike in soul and the possibility of infinite development."

The life of one of the most noteworthy figures in twentieth-century history is significant not just because of the drama revealed in it, but also because it is a story of the evolution—and occasional regression—of a brilliant man's thought. Du Bois' life tells another story as well; it epitomizes many of the tensions and problems inherent both in black leadership in the twentieth-century United States and in black day-to-day life.

William Edward Burghardt Du Bois was born on February 23, 1868, in Great Barrington, a quiet town in the Berkshire Mountains of western Massachusetts. His name provides clues to his racial heritage. He was born, Du Bois later recalled half in jest, half in bitterness, "with a flood of Negro blood, a strain of French, a bit of Dutch, but, thank God! no 'Anglo-Saxon'. . . ." As a boy, Du Bois was happy in Great Barrington. Although his family was relatively poor, his father having moved away and "faded out of our lives into silence" when Du Bois was very young, the lack of wealth was no insuperable obstacle to the enjoyment of childhood. Even race, for a while, was no handicap in this town with only fifty blacks. He had many white playmates, and he "saw the homes of nearly every one. . . . I think I probably surprised my hosts more than they me, for I was easily at home and perfectly happy and they looked to me just like ordinary people. . . ." With the approach of adolescence, however, this openness began to close.

"Very gradually," Du Bois wrote in an autobiographical essay, *Darkwater: Voices from Within the Veil* (1920), ". . . I found myself assuming quite placidly that I was different from other children." At first, he suspected that it was his superior schoolwork that set him apart from most of his schoolmates. "Then, slowly, I realized that some folks, a few, even several, actually considered my brown skin a misfortune; once or twice I became painfully aware that some human beings even thought it was a crime." Du Bois, writing in 1897, remembered vividly the first outright rejection of him as a person because of his race. The boys and girls in his "wee wooden schoolhouse" had decided "to buy gorgeous visiting cards" to exchange. "The exchange was merry, till one girl . . . refused my card—refused it peremptorily, with a glance. Then it dawned upon me with a certain suddenness that I was different from the others . . . shut out from their world by a vast veil. I had thereafter no desire to tear down that veil, to creep through. . . ." Being rejected only augmented Du Bois' urge to excel. "I was not for a moment daunted—although, of course, there were some days of secret tears—rather I was spurred to tireless effort. If they beat me at anything, I was grimly determined to make them sweat for it!"

Du Bois' race consciousness, which had begun to germinate during his adolescence, burst into full flower at Fisk University in Nashville, Tennessee. Originally, his dream—like that of many other sons of New England—had been to attend Harvard College. Having no money, however, Du Bois enrolled at Fisk in 1885, assisted by a scholarship funded by neighboring whites who felt that he would be happier among "his own people." At Fisk, he almost reveled in his blackness. "I am a Negro and I glory in the name!" he once exclaimed to his classmates in a public speech. "I am proud of the black blood that flows in my veins. From all the recollections dear to my childhood have I come here . . . to join hands with this, my people." At Fisk, Du Bois also resolved to become an essential member of that talented elite of college-educated black leaders who "were going to have these enslaved Israelites out of the still enduring bondage in short order." It was as an undergraduate, Du Bois recalled sixty years later, that "I replaced my hitherto egocentric world by a world centering and whirling about my race in America."

In the Tennessee landscape Du Bois also witnessed for the first time the outcropping of blatant racial intolerance and proscription. One summer Du Bois traveled to East Tennessee, where he "lived and taught in log cabins built before the Civil War." His school was only "the second held in the district since Emancipation." There, he noted, "I travelled not only in space but in time. I touched the very shadow of slavery." There he saw suffering: his people segregated in public accommodations, held in the bondage of perpetual debt, denied access to the ballot, to a jury trial by their peers, and to a decent education—and, on occasion, physically brutalized and even murdered.

Obviously upset by such suffering, Du Bois hoped to use his knowledge and skills to aid in the advancement of his race. Not desirous of miscegenation or "social equality"—that ill-defined but apocalyptic fear that afflicted many white Southerners—or perhaps even of integration, Du Bois merely wanted all people to have an equal opportunity for self-realization. Writing in a magazine article a decade later, Du Bois movingly conveyed the dilemma of the Afro-American, and thus of himself:

> One ever feels his two-ness—an American, a Negro; two souls, two thoughts, two unreconciled strivings; two warring ideals in one dark body, whose dogged strength alone keeps it from being torn asunder.

The history of the American Negro is the history of this strife,—this longing to attain self-conscious manhood, to merge his double self into a better and truer self. In this merging he wishes neither of the older selves to be lost. He does not wish to Africanize America, for America has too much to teach the world and Africa; he does not wish to bleach his Negro blood in a flood of white Americanism, for he believes . . . that Negro blood has yet a message for the world. He simply wishes to make it possible for a man to be both a Negro and an American without being cursed and spit upon by his fellows, without losing the opportunity of self-development.

In 1888, with a bachelor's degree from Fisk in hand, Du Bois entered Harvard College as a junior. Two years later he earned a Harvard B.A., and entered the university's graduate school. Having assured himself at Fisk that he was "a member of a closed racial group with rites and loyalties, with a history and a corporate future, with an art and philosophy," Du Bois arrived in Cambridge with "the theory of race separation . . . quite in my blood." Taking it for granted that Harvard's black and white students were preparing themselves "for different careers in worlds largely different," Du Bois "did not seek contact" with his "white fellow students. On the whole I rather avoided them." But on occasion, when avoidance was impossible, Du Bois found himself snubbed and rejected. His contacts with white faculty members, on the other hand, were often pleasurable and rewarding. He remembered being captivated by "the keen analysis" of William James, Josiah Royce, and George Santayana, and James he called "my favorite teacher and my closest friend." Moreover, it was James "with his pragmatism and Albert Bushnell Hart with his research method" who "turned me . . . to the social sciences as the field for gathering and interpreting that body of fact which would apply to my program for the Negro." The avenues of philosophy and history led him "to the study of sociology"; but since "Harvard recognized no 'science' of sociology," Du Bois, after vacillating between history and economics, selected history as his field of doctoral study. Having begun with a bibliography of the slave insurrection of Nat Turner, he concluded in 1895, after two years at the University of Berlin, with a doctoral dissertation entitled "The Suppression of the African Slave-Trade to the United States of America, 1638–1870," which was published the next year as the first volume in the *Harvard Historical Studies.*

Du Bois' two years in Europe, from 1892 to 1894, afforded a respite from the racism he so abhorred in the United States. "From the physical provincialism of America and the psychological provincialism of my rather narrow race problem into which I was born and which seemed to me the essence to life," Du Bois noted many years later, "I was transplanted and startled into a realization of the real centers of modern civilization and into at least a momentary escape from my own social problems. . . ." The obverse of his positive identity as an Afro-American was the negative identity he ascribed to the vast preponderance of whites; he took pride not only in being black but also in being non-white. But in Germany he temporarily "ceased to hate or suspect people simply because they belonged to one race or color. . . ."

Du Bois displayed another lifelong characteristic at this time—his proclivity for offending many black people by seeming to lecture down to them from a self-proclaimed position of intellectual superiority. This condescension was apparent in a speech he delivered to the National Colored League of Boston in 1891. He was alarmed, he told his audience, that "a people who have contributed nothing to modern civilization, who are largely on the lowest stages of barbarism in these closing days of the nineteenth century," should continue to neglect education. Referring caustically to "you people," he complained that while Ethiopia "is calling for the strong man, the master-felt man, the honest man, and the man who can forget himself," she has received instead a "reign of the coward." And his letters from Europe to the New York *Age*, a black newspaper, provoked the Cleveland *Gazette*, another black newspaper, to remark: "Much of W. E. B. Du Bois's letters from Europe published in the New York *Age* make one very tired. 'I, I, I, I, Me, me, me, Black bread and butter,' *Scat!*"

Sporting a Vandyke beard and a high silk hat, and bearing the affectations of the German student (gloves and a cane), the twenty-six-year-old Du Bois reinforced his image of haughtiness and aloofness as he arrived at his first American teaching position. Although only one year away from receiving his Harvard Ph.D., and having studied in Germany with some of the world's most eminent scholars (Adolf Wagner, Heinrich von Treitschke, Max Weber, and Gustav Schmoller), Du Bois, being black, apparently could not command the serious consideration of a predominantly white college or university. Instead, in August 1894, he traveled as professor of Greek and Latin to Ohio's Wilberforce College, a poor black school whose religious revivals and petty politics he soon found to be repugnant. Although a few of his students were of "first-class intelligence,

INTRODUCTION / 9

able and eager to work," most were "poorly equipped for study."
Even more frustrating to Du Bois was the school's unwillingness to
allow him to teach sociology. "I became uneasy about my life program," he recalled. "I was doing nothing directly in the social sciences and saw no immediate prospect. Then the door of opportunity
opened; just a crack, to be sure, but a distinct opening." In 1896
the provost of the University of Pennsylvania offered Du Bois a
special one-year fellowship as "Investigator of the Social Conditions
of the Colored Race" in Philadelphia's Seventh Ward slums. And
with his bride of a few months, Nina Gomer—"the slender, quiet,
and dark-eyed girl" who had been a student at Wilberforce—Du
Bois moved to Philadelphia.

Beginning with *The Philadelphia Negro* (1899) and continuing
through many articles and the annual Atlanta University conferences and *Publications* (Numbers 3–18, sixteen monographs published from 1898–1914), Du Bois dedicated himself to a scientific
study of Afro-American life. This basic research, he explained
several times, would not only disclose natural laws, but these laws,
in turn, would suggest programs of action. "The sole aim of any
society," Du Bois said in 1898, one year after moving to Atlanta
University, "is to settle its problems in accordance with its highest
ideals, and the only rational method of accomplishing this is to
study those problems in the light of the best scientific research."
From investigating such varied subjects as Africa, education, crime,
family life, the black businessman, artisan, farmer, and college student, "social betterment," and health among the nation's Afro-
Americans, Du Bois emerged with a comparatively conservative program of action for his race. Self-help, duty and discipline, efficiency,
thrift, intraracial economic cooperation, group pride, the responsibility of the black "aristocracy" to encourage and assist in the elevation of the black masses—these were among his charges to black
America. Of his white audience he urged interracial cooperation,
especially between the elite of both races, sympathetic understanding, the enlargement of opportunity for blacks, and recognition of
the fact that class and cultural distinctions existed among blacks
just as among whites.

"Be the Truth what it may," Du Bois had written on his twenty-
fifth birthday, "I shall seek it on the pure assumption that it is
worth seeking. . . ." Although it was in this spirit that Du Bois had
begun his scholarly investigations, he became dispirited. Never before had anyone gathered and organized so much data about blacks

in America; yet relatively few people, black or white, read his publications. Rather than engendering enthusiasm among white philanthropists and educators at black institutions, his research, which
was both action-oriented and a vehicle for expressing his commitment to the need for racial solidarity and the "exceptional" black
leader, often provoked hostility. But, most important, despite his
writings the oppression of Afro-Americans not only persisted but,
in certain ways, grew even more unbearable.

One exceedingly grotesque incident in particular caused him to
question the usefulness of his scholarly work. In various autobiographical writings, Du Bois recalled the lynching of Sam Hose
in Georgia in 1899. Accused of murdering his landlord's wife, Hose
was burned at the stake. "Before the torch was applied to the pyre,"
the New York *Tribune* reported, "the Negro was deprived of his
ears, fingers and other portions of his body. . . . Before the body
was cool, it was cut to pieces, the bones were crushed into small
bits," and pieces were hawked as souvenirs. "The Negro's heart was
cut in several pieces, as was also his liver. . . . Small pieces of bone
went for 25 cents and à bit of the liver, crisply cooked, for 10 cents."
Du Bois had hoped to prevent this outrage by preparing a "reasoned statement concerning the evident facts" for publication in
the Atlanta *Constitution*; naively, he seemed to believe that, were
the facts known, the lynchers would desist. But he never arrived at
the newspaper's offices with his report. "On the way news met me:
Sam Hose had been lynched, and they said that his knuckles were
on exhibition at a [nearby] grocery store. . . . I turned back to the
University. I began to turn aside from my work," morbidly aware
that "first, one could not be a calm, cool, and detached scientist
while Negroes were lynched, murdered and starved; and secondly,
there was no such definite demand for scientific work of the sort
that I was doing. . . ." Disillusioned, Du Bois began gradually to
espouse programs of direct action and to seek a wider audience for
his writings.

More and more, Du Bois would be an open propagandist for his
race, writing not only to stimulate a common consciousness among
blacks, but also to educate whites and, if possible, to shock them
into positive action; increasingly, his literary fruits would grace
the pages of mass-circulation magazines as well as those of erudite
journals. And, while not abandoning scholarship altogether, he
would begin to write popular books evoking the tragedy and the
beauty of being black in America. Moreover, politically he would

become an activist, protesting militantly for the civil rights of all of the nation's citizens. Several landmarks denote the journey Du Bois had undertaken: the publication of *The Souls of Black Folk* (1903); the organization of the Niagara Movement in 1905; and his assumption, in 1910, of the editorship of *The Crisis*.

Writing in the 1930's, the noted black composer, author, and civil rights leader James Weldon Johnson reflected that *The Souls of Black Folk* was "a work which, I think, has had a greater effect upon and within the Negro race in America than any other single book published in this country since *Uncle Tom's Cabin*." A collection of Du Bois' essays, the book's central thrust was a delineation of "the strange meaning of being black here at the dawning of the Twentieth Century"; understanding of "this meaning" was essential, Du Bois explained, "for the problem of the Twentieth Century is the problem of the color line,—the relation of the darker to the lighter races of men in Asia and Africa, in America and the islands of the sea." Blacks were separated from whites by "the Veil" of physical, emotional, social, economic, and political segregation. For Americans, and perhaps especially for white Americans, Du Bois had ventured to step "within the Veil, raising it that you may view faintly its deeper recesses"; and he had done so by discussing, among other things, slavery in America, Emancipation and Reconstruction, black life and race relations in the Southern "black belt," the significance of the church and education, African survivals in the New World, and the death of his infant son, his "First Born," who would not have "to cringe and bow" and suffer "a sea of sorrow."

One essay in particular, "Of Mr. Booker T. Washington and Others," stood out. Successor to Frederick Douglass as the nation's most prominent black, Washington was widely known as the principal of Alabama's Tuskegee Institute, but he was also an extremely influential Republican politician, the controller of large sums of white philanthropic money for black institutions, the leading spokesman for black capitalism and for "practical" rather than liberal arts education, the exerciser of almost dictatorial powers in black education, and a manipulator of other black leaders, newspapers, and organizations. "Easily the most striking thing in the history of the American Negro since 1876," Du Bois wrote, "is the ascendancy of Mr. Booker T. Washington." Du Bois conceded that while Washington had often employed his power for the benefit of the race, he had also stifled dissent in urging blacks to accommodate themselves to segregation and second-class citizenship, and had worked to crush the potential for racial advancement through the acquisition and use of the franchise and the development of a college-educated black leadership. "So far as Mr. Washington preaches Thrift, Patience, and Industrial Training for the masses," Du Bois concluded, "we must hold up his hands and strive with him. . . . But so far as Mr. Washington apologizes for injustice, North or South does not rightly value the privilege and duty of voting, belittles the emasculating effects of caste distinctions, and opposes the higher training and ambition of our brighter minds,—so far as he, the South, or the Nation, does this,—we must unceasingly and firmly oppose them."

In the opinion of James Weldon Johnson, the "chief significance" of Du Bois' essay on Washington lay "in the effect wrought by it within the race. It brought about a coalescence of the more radical elements and made them articulate, thereby creating a split of the race into two contending camps. . . ." Efforts at rapprochement between the Washington-led "conservatives" and the Du Bois-led "radicals" failed, in part because of the unwillingness of both sides to compromise over the issues of the vote and higher education. While appearing to be conciliatory, Washington instead mobilized the resources of his powerful "Tuskegee Machine" to overwhelm the opposition. "Things came to such a pass," Du Bois recalled later, "that when any Negro complained or advocated a course of action, he was silenced with the remark that Mr. Washington did not agree with this. Naturally, the bumptious, irritated, young black intelligentsia of the day declared, 'I don't care a damn what Booker Washington thinks! This is what I think and *I have a right to think.*'" Other Afro-Americans agreed; and in July 1905, Du Bois and twenty-eight other self-designated representatives of the college-educated "Talented Tenth" convened at Fort Erie, Ontario, to establish the Niagara Movement.

The Niagara Movement announced its principles in a "Declaration" written by Du Bois and William Monroe Trotter, the fiery editor of the Boston *Guardian*. Among these principles were: "freedom of speech and criticism"; a press "unfettered and unsubsidized" by the Tuskegee Machine; "manhood suffrage"; "the abolition of all caste distinctions based simply on race and color"; and "the recognition of the highest and best training as the monopoly of no class or race." "Are not all these things worth striving for?" Du Bois asked, and replied, *"The Niagara Movement* proposes to gain these ends." It proposed to do so, he reported, by agitating for political and civil rights, stimulating school construction and an "interest in education," opening up "new avenues of employment" and bringing "Negroes and labor unions into mutual understanding," attacking crime and disease so that black children could live and grow in an atmosphere of "physical and moral cleanliness," studying "Negro history," and, finally, by doing "all in our power by word or deed to increase the efficiency of our race, the enjoyment of its manhood rights, and the performance of its just duties."

After convening for five annual conferences, the Niagara Movement never met again. Always in financial difficulty, plagued with organizational problems and personality conflicts, and opposed at every step by Washington and his allies, the Niagara Movement had limped along from the beginning. But, as Elliott Rudwick has noted, it also took some significant steps. It was "the first national organization of Negroes which aggressively and unconditionally demanded the same civil rights for their people which other Americans enjoyed." Moreover, it had not only educated blacks to "a policy of protest," it had also "hewed a path for younger men [and women] to follow and helped to lay the foundation for the National Association for the Advancement of Colored People." In 1909–1910, Du Bois, who as Director of Publications and Research was the only black elected to national office in the NAACP, urged the other alumni of Niagara to enroll in the new organization.

Du Bois was not unhappy to leave Atlanta for New York in 1910 to assume the editorship of *The Crisis*. He had always felt like a stranger in the segregated city of Atlanta; and rather than allow himself to be discriminated against, he had simply abstained from riding the streetcars or going to the theaters or concert halls. Moreover, *The Crisis*, over which he would have virtually unrestricted editorial control, would be a much more influential vehicle for his views than his scholarly monographs had been. Du Bois would not be an organization man for the NAACP; he would be its public voice. "My career as a scientist," he later wrote, "was to be swallowed up in my role as master of propaganda. This was not wholly to my liking. . . . Nevertheless, having put my hand to the plow [in the Niagara Movement], I had to go on." And so he did, continuing to agitate for a combination of black self-development and a lessening of white hatred. Denouncing racial segregation, proscription, and other iniquities of "Anglo-Saxon civilization"; arguing that black people should be trained to work with their brains as well as with their hands, to feed their souls as well as their pocketbooks; and raging at white lynchers and espousing self-defense ("Let black men especially kill lecherous white invaders of their homes. . . ."), Du Bois edited and wrote trenchant articles for a monthly that by 1916 had a circulation of between 35,000–40,000, and by mid-1919 of over 100,000.

With American intervention in World War I, in April 1917, Du-Bois' editorials became less strident and more conciliatory. "If this is OUR country," he proclaimed, "then this is OUR war." Aligning himself with the Allies from the start, Du Bois rather inconsistently discounted the colonialism and racial oppression of England and France while warning that a German victory would mean "the triumph of every force calculated to subordinate darker peoples." Sharing President Wilson's idealism, Du Bois argued that victory would also result in the self-determination of oppressed peoples, and that it might even rid the world of the menace of future wars. Closer to home, Afro-Americans, by donning military uniforms and bearing arms, migrating from the rural South to Northern industrial centers, and learning new trades and earning higher wages, would begin to see "the walls of prejudice crumble before the onslaught of common sense and racial progress." In the summer of 1918, in "Close Ranks," Du Bois gave the war his unequivocal endorsement: "Let us, while this war lasts, forget our special grievances and close ranks shoulder to shoulder with our white fellow citizens. . . . We make no ordinary sacrifice, but we make it gladly and willingly, with our eyes lifted to the hills."

Du Bois did not still his voice entirely during the war (he protested bitterly, for example, against racial discrimination by the U.S. Civil Service Commission and the War Department), but his relative quiescence provoked criticism from other Afro-Americans, among them the editors of the Marxist-oriented journal *The Messenger,* Chandler Owen and A. Philip Randolph, who contended that "Close Ranks" would "rank in shame and reeking disgrace" with the most servile, self-serving statements of Booker T. Washington. But the years of the war were ones of confusion and ambivalence for Du Bois as well as for other black Americans, and the immediate postwar period only heightened Du Bois' uncertainty.

The year 1919, which was one of humiliation and bloodshed for black Americans, aroused in Du Bois numerous conflicting emotions and thoughts. Not only had the "walls of prejudice" not crumbled, but the incidence of lynchings and race riots soared during that

"Red Summer," leaving scores of black people dead. Labor unions and employers continued to discriminate, as did the army and other departments of the federal government. And the processes of war and peacemaking had not resulted in the overthrow of "white imperialism" by a system of self-determination for "darker peoples." As Du Bois' idealism and optimism waned, his disillusionment and anger soared. His disillusionment was evident in a story he wrote for the *Brownies' Book*, a black children's magazine he edited: "Fools, yes that's it. Fools. All of us fools fought a long, cruel, bloody and unnecessary war and we not only killed our boys—we killed Faith and Hope." His anger was evident in a *Crisis* editorial that gave voice to the militancy and determination of the war's black veterans:

> We *return*.
> We *return from fighting*.
> We *return fighting*.
> Make way for Democracy! We saved it in France, and by the Great Jehovah, we will save it in the United States of America, or know the reason why.

It was obvious in early 1919, as Du Bois and the fifty-six other worldwide "representatives of the Negro race" assembled in Paris for the Pan-African Congress, that his was "the loudest voice" in black America. Washington had died in 1915, but even before his death, and certainly by 1917, black leaders throughout the country had abandoned his policies and programs in favor of those advocated by Du Bois. "I think I may say without boasting," Du Bois later wrote, "that in the period from 1910 to 1930 I was a main factor in revolutionizing the attitude of the American Negro toward caste." Yet, as the black historian Lerone Bennett has noted, Du Bois was unlike Washington in that he "was not a natural leader." Du Bois himself conceded that he "could not easily break down an inhibited reserve," or always "curb" his "biting, critical tongue"; disdainful of "the essential demagoguery" of personal politics, he could not slap "people on the back and make friends of strangers." "As a result," Bennett writes, "Du Bois won influence, not power. His, as he said, was 'a leadership solely of ideas.' " So long as he oriented his ideas toward the destruction of segregation and second-class citizenship and toward the nurturing of racial equality and access to the "melting pot" for all Americans, his influence and authority were second to none in black America. But once he began publicly to advocate other routes to freedom and self-realization (for example, socialism, black nationalism, Pan-Africanism, and the development, not of racially integrated institutions, but of "self-separate" black economic, political, and educational ones), his influence and authority began to wane, until by 1934 he had severed his affiliation with the NAACP and resigned from the editorship of *The Crisis*.

For literally decades—at least since his undergraduate years at Fisk—central to Du Bois' ideological and philosophical commitments and predilections had been the concept of race: not merely the insistence, militant though it was, that race should not be a barrier to opportunity and fulfillment, but also the conviction that each race had its own special attributes and that these attributes should be preserved and perpetuated. Among the blacks' superior attributes, for example, were compassion, humanity, artistic sensitivity ("We are the only American artists," wrote Du Bois), and physical grace and loveliness. Rather than aping whites, Du Bois urged Afro-Americans to derive beauty and substance from their own heritage and culture. The Afro-American race, Du Bois wrote in 1916, should emulate the "old ideals . . . [the] old standards of beauty . . . not the blue eyed, white skinned types which are set before us in school and literature but rich, brown and black men and women with glowing dark eyes and crinkling hair . . . that harks back to the heritage of Africa and the tropics." Du Bois could thus fight against both the legislation that forbade intermarriage (for such laws demeaned blacks) and the institution itself (for it diluted the black race). But if the obverse of an attribute is a defect, then Du Bois, by ascribing negative characteristics to the entire white race, was vulnerable to accusations of "black chauvinism" and racism in reverse. Du Bois asserted in 1913, for example, that it was instinctive for "the most ordinary Negro" to be a gentleman, but "it takes extraordinary training, gift and opportunity to make the average white man anything but an overbearing hog." Such statements, quite obviously, were at odds with the integrationist platform of the NAACP.

Pan-Africanism, not a new commitment for Du Bois, became one of his primary activities in the 1920's. He had attended the 1900 Pan-African Conference in London, and he had traveled again to that city in 1911 for the Universal Races Congress. He was a key functionary at the 1919 Pan-African Congress, and again in 1921,

1923, and 1927. In 1923 and early 1924, Du Bois made his first visit to Africa, "the Eternal World of Black Folk," which he said was the "greatest" event of his life. To Du Bois, the crucial "question" was "whether Negroes are to lead in the rise of Africa or whether they must always and everywhere follow the guidance of white folk." Much to his distress, the Pan-African movement of the 1920's did not provide the answer; but like the Niagara Movement of twenty years before, it did set a valuable precedent—in this case, for the 1945 Pan-African Congress attended by Du Bois, Nkrumah, Jomo Kenyatta, George Padmore, and others.

Also throughout the 1920's, Du Bois became ever more doubtful about the efficacy of his earlier programs for racial advancement. Having beseeched blacks not to acquiesce in the establishment or perpetuation of segregated classrooms, he now began to criticize desegregated school systems where black children would be "abused, browbeaten, murdered, and kept in something worse than ignorance." He also expressed his lack of confidence in the Talented Tenth of college students, condemning them for elitism, "snobbishness," and for becoming a "closed clan" distinct from the black masses. The "black college man today," Du Bois charged puritanically, not only "deliberately surrenders to selfish and even silly ideals" (for example, Greek-letter fraternities and "semi-professional athletics"), but he has also become a conspicuous and "vulgar" consumer of "liquor, extravagance, and fur coats." Rather than young men and women dedicated to the uplift of the race, "we have in our colleges," Du Bois wrote, "a growing mass of stupidity and indifference." The students, however, were not solely accountable, for the colleges had not observed their duty to teach about the economic system, especially its manufacturing and distributive components. In a proposal reminiscent of Booker T. Washington, Du Bois suggested an expansion of the college curriculum to encompass "vocational training" and "industrial planning" as well as the liberal arts. For both "education and work," he insisted in 1930, were crucial functions of the black college, which should be a "center of applied knowledge and guide of action," training industrial technicians *and* a leadership of "exceptional men." Heretofore, black college graduates had become part of "a white collar proletariat, depending for their support on [a black] economic foundation which does not exist"; and it was now crucial to construct that foundation.

While Du Bois did not renounce politics in the 1920's, he contended that black political action could wrest from the white power structure only concessions, not solutions. Blacks had to combat an essentially economic problem with economic weapons; and it was in the articulation of his solution—a "closed [black] economic circle"—that Du Bois embarked upon a course that would eventually isolate him from the NAACP. Always critical of capitalism for "its racial overtones and its class exploitation," Du Bois advocated the establishment of black manufacturing and consumers' cooperatives. How would the "closed economic circle" function? As outlined by one of Du Bois' biographers: "Raw materials drawn from Negro farmers, transported by Negro trucks and turned into finished products in Negro factories, would eventually find their way to intelligent and loyal Negro customers who patronized Negro cooperative stores." But was this not a kind of "voluntary segregation"? Perhaps it was, Du Bois conceded, but, first of all, racial segregation was an inescapable reality of American life and, second, racial pride and freedom from "economic slavery" dictated such a course. Moreover, Du Bois contended, the only substantive racial progress of the past twenty-five years had been the product of all-black endeavors and institutions, and, he added pessimistically, "there seems no hope that [white] America in our day will yield in its color or race hatred any substantial ground and we have no physical nor economic power, nor any alliance with other social or economic classes that will force compliance with decent civilized ideals in Church, State, industry or art."

In addition to the hopelessness of "looking for salvation from the whites," Du Bois began in 1929 and 1930 to assess the devastating consequences of the Great Depression for black America. Although the entire country was being ravaged by economic diseases, dying black banks and businesses fell faster and harder than white institutions, and blacks suffered disproportionately from unemployment, hunger, and despair. "In a world where economic dislocation had become so great as in ours," Du Bois wrote, "a mere appeal based on the old liberalism, a mere appeal to justice . . . was missing the essential need," which was "to guard and better the chances of Negroes, educated and ignorant, to earn a living, safeguard their income, and raise the level of their employment." With these words, and with his advocacy of a socialized all-black economy, Du Bois abandoned most of his programs of the past several decades. He rejected the traditional integrationist approach to civil rights because of the implacability of racism in America; he rejected the concept of an interracial socialized society, in which blue-collar blacks and whites would unite against white capitalism, because of the racism of white workers and their unions; and he rejected the idea of the Talented Tenth because an "aristocracy" of brains, like any aristocracy, would neglect and even betray the masses. In the early 1930's, as Francis Broderick has observed, "Du Bois turned to the only allies on whom he felt the Negro could count: his twelve million Negro fellow Americans." Many contemporary observers, however, made a harsh appraisal of Du Bois' alleged "retreat." He had become an accommodationist, they charged, abandoning the struggle for first-class citizenship and embracing Washington's philosophy of "uplift" through vocational education, nonprotest, and black economic enterprise.

Compounding his ideological disputes with the NAACP were Du Bois' personality conflicts with other NAACP officials, especially Walter F. White, the executive secretary, and the deteriorating health of *The Crisis,* which had been operating at an annual deficit of several thousand dollars since the mid-1920's. With the magazine no longer self-supporting, Du Bois had had to request in 1929 and 1930 a subsidy from the NAACP's national board. The board, in granting the funds, had decreed that, thereafter, editorial policy would be exercised not by Du Bois alone, but by a committee of four. With financial dependence, the board had voted, there could no longer be unrestricted editorial independence. Yet Du Bois persisted in trumpeting the virtues of "self-segregation" and the "closed economic circle"; in disputing the NAACP's policies (writing in the April 1934, *Crisis* issue that "the net result" of the NAACP's twenty-five-year "campaign against segregation . . . has been a little less than nothing"); and even in ridiculing its leaders (writing in the same issue, for example, that the very light-skinned Walter White "has more white companions and friends than colored . . . , for the simple and sufficient reason that he isn't 'colored'. . . ."). By 1934 Du Bois' position was totally untenable, and in June of that year he resigned from the editorship. He had concluded that, after a quarter of a century, he would resume his teaching and scholarship at Atlanta University.

The news of Du Bois' resignation elicited a response that must have been painful to such a proud man. In what apparently was the majority opinion of black America, the militantly integrationist Chicago *Defender* published photographs of Washington and Du Bois. Over that of Washington, it mused sorrowfully: "WAS HE

RIGHT AFTER ALL?" Over that of Du Bois: "IS HE A QUITTER?"

At the age of sixty-six, when most men were settling into un-eventful retirement, Du Bois, for the second time, embarked upon an academic career. And, as before, the cool and fastidious demeanor of Professor Du Bois masked the passion of his pen. In late 1934, for example, he finished the writing of a monumental book, *Black Reconstruction in America,* a Marxist interpretation of Recon-struction that broke new ground in shifting the focus to social and economic developments and carried the lengthy but graphic subtitle, *An Essay Toward a History of the Part Which Black Folk Played in the Attempt to Reconstruct Democracy in America, 1860–1880.* Five years later he established the journal *Phylon,* Atlanta Uni-versity's "Review of Race and Culture," which he said was, "in a sense," a revival of the Atlanta University *Publications.* In 1939 and 1940 two more books were published: *Black Folk, Then and Now,* an expanded version of *The Negro* (1915), and *Dusk of Dawn,* an autobiographical essay that examined his ideological journey from civil rights protest to Marxism and to the concept of economic self-sufficiency for "the colored world within" the white world. And, as he had done over forty years before, he initiated a systematic investigation of the status of black people; this, he ambitiously re-ported in 1943, would be a "total study of a complete situation as a contribution to the Negro race, America, the world, and social science."

But scholarship and teaching were insufficient to sustain either Du Bois' energies or his commitment to fundamental change in the United States and throughout the world; it was obvious that even in academe he would persist in being a propagandist for both Afro-America and Marxism. Truth, he wrote in 1939, was still the "cause I seek to serve, and wherever I fail, I am at least paying the Truth the respect of earnest effort." He was frank to confess, how-ever, that he could not always be objective, and that at times he had to resort to "conjecture and even . . . guesswork." Even if he had to be a polemicist, he could not acquiesce in the depiction of the Afro-American as "the clown of history; the football of an-thropology; and the slave of industry"; it was unbearable that white scholars, writers, and other "champions of white folks" should be acknowledged as the experts on black America. In 1944 Du Bois wrote an article entitled "Phylon: Science or Propaganda." Asserting that Afro-American progress from slavery to the present had been "the greatest controlled laboratory test of the science of human action in the world," Du Bois deplored the fact that the history of this progress had been distorted and demeaned. If it were propagandistic to correct this imbalance, Du Bois concluded, then "we're propagandists."

At this time Du Bois also resolved many of his uncertainties about Marxism in general and Russian communism in particular. Philosophically and emotionally committed for years to socialism, Du Bois had been a member of the Socialist Party for one year, in 1911; and in 1907, referring to himself as a "Socialist-of-the-path," he had predicted that "we are approaching a time when the railroads, coal mines, and many factories can and ought to be run by the public for the public. . . ." Blacks should not pursue the capitalistic goals of "wealth, power, oppression, and snobbishness," but rather the socialistic goals of "helpfulness, efficiency, service, and self-respect. Watch the Socialists," he urged. "We may not follow them and agree with them in all things. I certainly do not. But in trend and ideal they are the salt of this present earth."

At first Du Bois had been ambivalent about the Russian Revolution of 1917. It was unwise for black Americans, he wrote in 1921, "to join a revolution which we do not at present understand"; but a year later, he acclaimed the Russian Revolution as "the most amazing and most hopeful phenomenon" in the postwar world. And in 1926, his expenses having been paid by a man who, Du Bois surmised, was probably a "clandestine" agent of the "communist dictatorship," he made his first trip to the Soviet Union. Initially skeptical, Du Bois returned to the United States in awe of what he had witnessed. "I stand in astonishment and wonder," he wrote in *The Crisis,* "at the revelation of Russia that has come to me. I may be partially deceived and half-informed. But if what I have seen with my own eyes and heard with my own ears in Russia is Bolshevism, I am a Bolshevik."

Du Bois' "Bolshevism," however, did not immediately extend to the Communist Party of the United States. He still believed, as he had in the early 1920's, that blacks, rather than being the beneficiaries of working-class solidarity with whites, were more often the victims of "physical oppression, social ostracism, economic exclusion and personal hatred on the part of the white proletariat." And in the early 1930's Du Bois responded angrily to the Communist accusation that it was the NAACP's "Negro bourgeois reformism" that was the "main social bulwark of imperialist Jim Crow reaction among the Negro masses." For their part, Du Bois wrote, the Communists had cynically exploited "the poorest and most ignorant blacks, head[ing] them toward inevitable slaughter and jail slavery, while they [the Communists] hide safely. . . . American Negroes," Du Bois declared, "do not propose to be the shock troops of the Communist Revolution, driven out in front to death, cruelty and humiliation in order to win victories for white workers. They are picking no chestnuts from the fire, neither for capital nor white labor."

By the later 1930's Du Bois had shifted the focus of his energies and intellect away from the evil of domestic racism and onto what he saw as the twin evils of worldwide capitalism and imperialism. Increasingly, as he analyzed American foreign policy and that of other nations, he employed two criteria: "Had the nation moved toward a socialistic organization of society? Was it nonimperialistic, that is, was it a white nation free of the taint of extending political or economic control over a darker people?" Judged by these criteria, Russia was "highly favored," while the United States, Great Britain, and other Western nations were castigated as exploitative enemies of self-determination and world peace.

In 1944, after being retired by Atlanta University, Du Bois was invited by the NAACP to direct "special research" projects on race relations and international affairs. Du Bois' rehiring by the NAACP (allegedly because Walter White at this time remembered Du Bois' contributions to "straight thinking by the Negro") was as surprising as Atlanta's sudden termination of his teaching contract (apparently because of Du Bois' public criticism of the university's educational policies and the propagandistic tone of *Phylon*) was mysterious. But for Du Bois this was an invitation to step again into the political arena, and this time to perform before a worldwide audience. Moving again to New York City, the seventy-six-year-old Du Bois announced that the problem of imperialism, with its attendant economic, political, and social suppression of colonial peoples, was "the problem to which I propose to devote the remaining years of my active life."

Although his affiliation with the NAACP enabled him to serve as an associate consultant to the American delegation at the 1945 San Francisco Conference to draft the United Nations Charter, Du Bois was prompt to condemn the proceedings, which, he charged, had effectively precluded the representation of 750,000,000 subject peoples in the international organization. Du Bois also served in 1945 as International President of the Pan-African Congress in England; here, too, the fundamental issue was Western imperialism. In 1947 he journeyed again to the United Nations to petition ("An Appeal to the World") for the exertion of worldwide pressure on the United States "to be just to its own [nonwhite] peoples." The Soviet Union endorsed a hearing on the "Appeal," but the effort was resisted by the United States. Already the Cold War was a reality; and Du Bois, in reviling "the reactionary, war-mongering colonial administration of the present [Truman] administration," had clearly become a partisan of revolutionary socialism.

Because of this statement in 1948 and, additionally, because he had promoted the left-wing presidential candidacy of the Progressive Party's Henry Wallace, Du Bois was fired by the pro-Truman Administration NAACP. The hysterically antiradical and paranoiac era of "McCarthyism" was about to engulf the United States, and Du Bois, being progressively anti-American and pro-Russian in the Cold War struggle, had committed himself to the unpopular minority. In 1948 he became vice-chairman of the Council on African Affairs, an organization that the U.S. Attorney General had cited as "subversive." Writing now almost exclusively for such left-wing publications as *Masses and Mainstream, New Africa,* and the *National Guardian,* Du Bois denounced what he and others on the Left judged to be American imperialism: "Drunk with power, we [the United States] are leading the world to hell in a new colonialism with the same old human slavery which once ruined us and to a third world war which will ruin the world." In 1949 he was in Moscow for the All-Union Conference of Peace Proponents, and in New York and Paris for other meetings of the international "peace crusade." In 1950 he traveled to Prague as a guest of the World Congress of the Defenders of Peace. Furthermore, in 1950 Du Bois, for the first time, ventured into elective politics, as the American Labor Party's candidate for the U.S. Senate from New York. His campaign pronouncements, however, were totally in conflict with the prevailing Cold War ideology of thoroughgoing American "innocence" and Russian "guilt" for war, revolution, and international tension. Declaring that his candidacy was the only alternative to the Democratic and Republican "bipartisan policy of war," Du Bois went down to overwhelming defeat in November.

By 1951 McCarthyism was a threat not only to the nation's colleges and universities, labor unions, movie industry, and political,

religious, and civic organizations, but also to the fundamental free-
doms of speech and association. In February of that year—indeed,
one year to the day after Senator Joseph R. McCarthy had first
proclaimed that he had in his possession the names of numerous
State Department officials who were card-carrying members of the
Communist Party—Du Bois fell victim to this modern "know-
nothingism," having been indicted by a federal grand jury for
being an unregistered "agent of a foreign principal." His primary
offense, according to the indictment, was that, as chairman of the
Peace Information Center, he had been instrumental in circulating
the "Stockholm Peace Appeal," an eighty-word petition that advocated the absolute prohibition of atomic weapons. Several months
earlier, Secretary of State Dean Acheson had labeled the petition a
"propaganda trick in the spurious 'peace offensive' of the Soviet
Union," and the House Un-American Activities Committee, ever
paranoid about the "traitors" within, had condemned it as "Communist chicanery." Undeterred, Du Bois had responded by noting
that one million Americans had already signed the document, and
by querying whether Acheson's statement signified that "there is no
possibility of mediating our differences with Russia."

Du Bois' five-day trial began on November 8, 1951, and although
the judge entered a verdict of acquittal, the ordeal accelerated the
pace of Du Bois' estrangement from the United States. Francis
Broderick has written that the trial was "an epochal moment" in
Du Bois' career, even more significant than his resignation from
The Crisis in 1934. For if "there was a sharp break in Du Bois' ideas,
it came not in 1934, when he separated from the [NAACP]," but
in 1952 when "he abandoned race and aligned his hopes with the
world forces that he saw to be fighting for peace and for the working classes. In Du Bois's view these world forces were best represented by Russia."

While Du Bois subordinated the issue of race in America to
that of world socialism in the 1950's, it would be erroneous to state
that he had "abandoned" the issue. In the 1950's, Du Bois, who was
a very old but still alert and lucid man in his late eighties and early
nineties, traveled to Russia, the People's Republic of China, East
Germany, Czechoslovakia, Poland, and Rumania. But he was still
curious about and probing into the state of American race relations
and the status of Afro-Americans. Astonished by the Supreme Court's
1954 school desegregation ruling, he exclaimed: "I have seen the
impossible happen." The 1960 lunch-counter sit-ins exhilarated him,

for these were black students, "not agitators, not even radicals . . . just honest, clear-headed youth." Even so, he was at times so pessimistic about the prospect of ultimate liberation for America's black people that he could declare, as he did in 1956: "Democracy is dead in the United States." And to the extent that he did envisage liberation, he saw it as one of the indispensable by-products of a world socialist and anti-imperialist revolution.

On October 1, 1961, at the age of ninety-three, Du Bois made application for membership in the Communist Party of the United States. "I have been long and slow in coming to this conclusion," he wrote Gus Hall, the party's general secretary, "but at last my mind is settled." Recounting his gradual conversion, Du Bois announced that, "[today] I have reached a firm conclusion: Capitalism cannot reform itself; it is doomed to self-destruction." Communism, on the other hand, "is the only way of human life," and, "in the end," it "will triumph. I want to help bring that day." Also in late 1961 Du Bois accepted President Kwame Nkrumah's offer to reside in Ghana and to supervise research for the government-sponsored *Encyclopaedia Africana*. In February 1963, just six months before his death at ninety-five, Du Bois became a Ghanaian citizen.

On August 28, 1963, there assembled in Washington 250,000 people, most of them black. Awaiting the beginning of the march from the Washington Monument to the Lincoln Memorial, these men, women, and children were joyful and they were united. "I Was There," read the buttons worn by thousands of the Marchers On Washington; this was a day they intended not to forget. Many picnicked, having brought with them luncheon baskets, thermos jugs, and camp stools. Some stretched out to rest on the grass. High-school students improvised dances, clapped hands, and sang freedom songs. Though the marchers were joyful, their cause—civil rights for America's black citizens—was deadly serious; they demanded "freedom" and they demanded it "now." Over the powerful amplification system came the voice of Ossie Davis, the black actor, announcing that the day before, in Ghana, W. E. B. Du Bois had died. In tribute thousands upon thousands of people stood momentarily silent, their heads bowed.

Seven years before, Du Bois had composed his own eulogy. He had "loved" his work, he had written, and "I have loved people and my play, but always I have been uplifted by the thought that what I have done well will live long and justify my life. . . . And that peace will be applause." Concluding this "Last Message to the

World," Du Bois had left one charge to its people:

> As you live, believe in life! Always human beings will live and progress to greater, broader and fuller life.
>
> The only possible death is to lose belief in this truth simply because the great end comes slowly, because time is long.
>
> Good-bye.

Chronology of the Life and Major Works of W. E. B. Du Bois

1868	February 23, born in Great Barrington, Massachusetts.
1885–88	Attends Fisk University (B.A.).
1888	Enters Harvard as a junior, being graduated with a B.A. (1890).
1892–94	Studies at the University of Berlin.
1896	Awarded the Ph.D. by Harvard, his doctoral dissertation (*The Suppression of the African Slave Trade to the United States of America, 1638–1870*) being published as Volume I in "Harvard Historical Studies."
1894–96	Professor of Greek and Latin, Wilberforce College, Ohio; marries Nina Gomer, a Wilberforce student.
1896–97	Assistant Instructor in Sociology, University of Pennsylvania, conducting research for *The Philadelphia Negro: A Social Study* (1899).
1897–1910	Professor of Economics and History, Atlanta University; organizer of the Atlanta University Conference's "Studies of the Negro Problem" and editor of the Conference's annual *Publications*.
1903	Publishes *The Souls of Black Folk*.
1905–09	Becomes a founder and the General Secretary of the Niagara Movement.
1906	Founds and edits *The Moon Illustrated Weekly*.
1907–10	Founds and edits *The Horizon: A Journal of the Color Line*.
1909	Publishes *John Brown*.
1910	Among the founders of the National Association for the Advancement of Colored People, serving (1910–34) as the NAACP's Director of Publicity and Research and as editor of *The Crisis*.
1911	Publishes *The Quest of the Silver Fleece* (a novel).
1915	Publishes *The Negro*.
1919	Chief organizer of the Pan-African Congress (also organizing and attending meetings of the Congress in 1921, 1923, and 1927).
1920	Publishes *Darkwater*.
1920–21	Founds and edits *The Brownies' Book*, a magazine for children.
1923–24	Makes first trip to Africa.
1924	Publishes *The Gift of Black Folk*.

1926	Makes first trip to the Soviet Union.
1928	Publishes *Dark Princess* (a novel).
1934	Resigns from the editorship of *The Crisis* and from the Board of the NAACP, returning to Atlanta University as Chairman of the Department of Sociology (1934–44).
1935	Publishes *Black Reconstruction in America, 1860–1880.*
1939	Publishes *Black Folk, Then and Now.*
1940	Founds and edits (to 1944) *Phylon.*
1940	Publishes *Dusk of Dawn: An Essay toward an Autobiography of a Race Concept.*
1944	Returns to NAACP (until 1948) as Director of Special Research.
1945	Consultant to the Founding Convention of the United Nations, San Francisco; presides at the Fifth Pan-African Congress, Manchester, England.
1945	Publishes *Encyclopedia of the Negro: Preparatory Volume.*
1945	Publishes *Color and Democracy: Colonies and Peace.*
1947	Editor of the NAACP's *An Appeal to the World . . . ,* for presentation to the United Nations.
1947	Publishes *The World and Africa.*
1948	Vice-Chairman, Council on African Affairs.
1950	Chairman, Peace Information Center; American Labor Party candidate for U.S. Senator from New York; wife, Nina Gomer Du Bois, dies.
1951	Federal indictment, trial, and acquittal on charges of being an "unregistered foreign agent."
1952	Marries writer Shirley Graham.
1952	Publishes *In Battle for Peace: The Story of My 83rd Birthday.*
1957–61	Publishes *The Black Flame—A Trilogy: The Ordeal of Mansart* (1957), *Mansart Builds a School* (1959), and *Worlds of Color* (1961).
1958–59	Extensive travels to "Iron Curtain" countries.
1961	Joins the Communist Party of the United States; at the invitation of President Kwame Nkrumah, becomes a resident of Ghana and Director of the *Encyclopaedia Africana.*
1963	Publishes *An ABC of Color.*
1963	Becomes a citizen of Ghana, dying there on August 27, 1963.
1968	*The Autobiography of W. E. B. Du Bois: A Soliloquy on Viewing My Life from the Last Decade of Its First Century* is published posthumously.

W. E. B. DU BOIS LOOKS AT BLACK AMERICA AND THE WORLD

1

Thoughts and Ideas at the Turn of the Twentieth Century

During the closing years of the nineteenth century and the opening years of the twentieth, W. E. B. Du Bois enunciated most of the ideas that would distinguish his thought for the remaining years of his life. Among these ideas were the concept of the "two-ness" of Afro-American life, including a commitment to both first-class citizenship and the "conservation" of radical identity and integrity; racial pride and all-black group action; the "Talented Tenth"; the necessity of agitation and propaganda to gain political, economic, and social equality of opportunity; the preservation and perpetuation of black art, culture, and history; Pan-Africanism; and socialism.

THE "TWO-NESS" OF THE AFRO-AMERICAN EXPERIENCE [1]

Between me and the other world there is ever an unasked question: unasked by some through feelings of delicacy; by others through the difficulty of rightly framing it. All, nevertheless, flutter round it. They approach me in a half-hesitant sort of way, eye me curiously or compassionately, and then, instead of saying directly, How does it feel to be a problem? they say, I know an excellent

[1] "Strivings of the Negro People," *Atlantic Monthly,* LXXX (August 1897), 194–98. This article became Chapter I of *The Souls of Black Folk: Essays and Sketches* (Chicago: A. C. McClurg & Co., 1903), pp. 1–12.

colored man in my town; . . . or, Do not these Southern outrages make your blood boil? At these I smile, or am interested, or reduce the boiling to a simmer, as the occasion may require. To the real question, How does it feel to be a problem? I answer seldom a word.

And yet, being a problem is a strange experience,—peculiar even for one who has never been anything else, save perhaps in babyhood and in Europe. It is in the early days of rollicking boyhood that the revelation first bursts upon one, all in a day, as it were. . . . Then it dawned upon me with a certain suddenness that I was different from the others; or like, mayhap, in heart and life and longing, but shut out from their world by a vast veil. I had thereafter no desire to tear down that veil, to creep through; I held all beyond it in common contempt, and lived above it in a region of blue sky and great wandering shadows. That sky was bluest when I could beat my mates at examination-time, or beat them at a foot-race, or even beat their stringy heads. Alas, with the years all this fine contempt began to fade; for the world I longed for, and all its dazzling opportunities, were theirs, not mine. But they should not keep these prizes, I said; some, all, I would wrest from them. Just how I would do it I could never decide: by reading law, by healing the sick, by telling the wonderful tales that swam in my head,—some way. With other black boys the strife was not so fiercely sunny: their youth shrunk into tasteless sycophancy, or into silent hatred of the pale world about them and mocking distrust of everything white; or wasted itself in a bitter cry, Why did God make me an outcast and a stranger in mine own house? The "shades of the prisonhouse" closed round about us all: walls strait and stubborn to the whitest, but relentlessly narrow, tall, and unscalable to sons of night who must plod darkly on in resignation, or beat unavailing palms against the stone, or steadily, half hopelessly watch the streak of blue above.

After the Egyptian and Indian, the Greek and Roman, the Teuton and Mongolian, the Negro is a sort of seventh son, born with a veil, and gifted with second-sight in this American world,—a world which yields him no self-consciousness, but only lets him see himself through the revelation of the other world. It is a peculiar sensation, this double-consciousness, this sense of always looking at one's self through the eyes of others, of measuring one's soul by the tape of a world that looks on in amused contempt and pity. One ever feels his two-ness,—an American, a Negro; two souls, two thoughts, two unreconciled strivings; two warring ideals in one dark body, whose dogged strength alone keeps it from being torn asunder. The history of the American Negro is the history of this strife,—this longing to attain self-conscious manhood, to merge his double self into a better and truer self. In this merging he wishes neither of the older selves to be lost. He does not wish to Africanize America, for America has too much to teach the world and Africa; he does not wish to bleach his Negro blood in a flood of white Americanism, for he believes— foolishly, perhaps, but fervently—that Negro blood has yet a message for the world. He simply wishes to make it possible for a man to be both a Negro and an American without being cursed and spit upon by his fellows, without losing the opportunity of self-development.

This is the end of his striving: to be a co-worker in the kingdom of culture, to escape both death and isolation, and to husband and use his best powers. These powers, of body and of mind, have in the past been so wasted and dispersed as to lose all effectiveness, and to seem like absence of all power, like weakness. . . .

This waste of double aims, this seeking to satisfy two unreconciled ideals, has wrought sad havoc with the courage and faith and deeds of eight thousand thousand people, has sent them often wooing false gods and invoking false means of salvation, and has even at times seemed destined to make them ashamed of themselves. In the days of bondage they thought to see in one divine event the end of all doubt and disappointment; eighteenth-century Rousseauism never worshiped freedom with half the unquestioning faith that the American Negro did for two centuries. To him slavery was, indeed, the sum of all villainies, the cause of all sorrow, the root of all prejudice; emancipation was the key to a promised land of sweeter beauty than ever stretched before the eyes of wearied Israelites. In his songs and exhortations swelled one refrain, liberty; in his tears and curses the god he implored had freedom in his right hand. At last it came,— suddenly, fearfully, like a dream. With one wild carnival of blood and passion came the message in his own plaintive cadences:—

> "Shout, O children!
>   Shout, you're free!
> The Lord has bought your liberty!"

Years have passed away, ten, twenty, thirty. Thirty years of national life, thirty years of renewal and development, and yet the . . . freedman has not yet found in freedom his promised land. Whatever of lesser good may have come in these years of change, the shadow of a deep disappointment rests upon the Negro people,—a disappointment all the more bitter because the unattained ideal was un-bounded save by the simple ignorance of a lowly folk.

. . . The ideals of physical freedom, of political power, of school training, as separate all-sufficient panaceas for social ills, became in the third decade [since Emancipation] dim and overcast. They were the vain dreams of credulous race childhood; not wrong, but in-complete and over-simple. The training of the schools we need to-day more than ever,—the training of deft hands, quick eyes and ears, and the broader, deeper, higher culture of gifted minds. The power of the ballot we need in sheer self-defense, and as a guarantee of good faith. We may misuse it, but we can scarce do worse in this respect than our whilom masters. Freedom, too, the long-sought, we still seek,—the freedom of life and limb, the freedom to work and think. Work, culture, and liberty,—all these we need, not singly, but together; for to-day these ideals among the Negro people are gradually coalescing, and finding a higher meaning in the unifying ideal of race,—the ideal of fostering the traits and talents of the Negro, not in opposition to, but in conformity with, the greater ideals of the American republic, in order that some day, on Ameri-can soil, two world races may give each to each those characteristics which both so sadly lack. Already we come not altogether empty-handed: there is to-day no true American music but the sweet wild melodies of the Negro slave; the American fairy tales are Indian and African; we are the sole oasis of simple faith and reverence in a dusty desert of dollars and smartness. Will America be poorer if she replace her brutal, dyspeptic blundering with the light-hearted but determined Negro humility; or her coarse, cruel wit with loving, jovial good humor; or her Annie Rooney with Steal Away?

Merely a stern concrete test of the underlying principles of the great republic is the Negro problem, and the spiritual striving of the freedmen's sons is the travail of souls whose burden is almost beyond the measure of their strength, but who bear it in the name of an historic race, in the name of this the land of their fathers' fathers, and in the name of human opportunity.

ON THE NEED FOR THE "CONSERVATION" OF RACIAL IDENTITY AND FOR RACIAL GROUP ORGANIZATION AND ACTION [2]

The American Negro has always felt an intense personal interest in discussions as to the origins and destinies of races: primarily because back of most discussions of race with which he is familiar, have lurked certain assumptions as to his natural abilities, as to his political, intellectual and moral status, which he felt were wrong. He has, consequently, been led to deprecate and minimize race distinctions, to believe intensely that out of one blood God created all nations, and to speak of human brotherhood as though it were the possibility of an already dawning to-morrow.

Nevertheless, in our calmer moments we must acknowledge that human beings are divided into races; that in this country the two most extreme types of the world's races have met, and the resulting problem as to the future relations of these types is not only of intense and living interest to us, but forms an epoch in the history of mankind.

. . . The question, then, which we must seriously consider is this: What is the real meaning of Race; what has, in the past, been the law of race development, and what lessons has the past history of race development to teach the rising Negro people? . . .

Although the wonderful developments of human history teach that the grosser physical differences of color, hair and bone go but a short way toward explaining the different roles which groups of men have played in Human Progress, yet there are differences—subtle, delicate and elusive, though they may be—which have silently but definitely separated men into groups. While these subtle forces have generally followed the natural cleavage of common blood, descent and physical peculiarities, they have at other times swept across and ignored these. At all times, however, they have divided human beings into races, which, while they perhaps transcend scientific definition, nevertheless, are clearly defined to the eye of the Historian and Sociologist.

If this be true, then the history of the world is the history, not of individuals, but of groups, not of nations, but of races, and he who ignores or seeks to override the race idea in human history ignores and overrides the central thought of all history. What, then, is a

[2] *The Conservation of Races* (Washington, D.C.: The American Negro Academy [Occasional Papers, No. 2], 1897), pp. 5–15.

race? It is a vast family of human beings, generally of common blood and language, always of common history, traditions and impulses, who are both voluntarily and involuntarily striving together for the accomplishment of certain more or less vividly conceived ideals of life.

Turning to real history, there can be no doubt, first, as to the widespread, nay, universal, prevalence of the race idea, the race spirit, the race ideal, and as to its efficiency as the vastest and most ingenious invention for human progress. We, who have been reared and trained under the individualistic philosophy of the Declaration of Independence and the laisser-faire philosophy of Adam Smith, are loath to see and loath to acknowledge this patent fact of human history. . . . We are apt to think in our American impatience, that while it may have been true in the past that closed race groups made history, that here in conglomerate America . . . we have changed all that, and have no need of this ancient instrument of progress. This assumption of which the Negro people are especially fond, can not be established by a careful consideration of history.

We find upon the world's stage today eight distinctly differentiated races, in the sense in which History tells us the word must be used. They are, the Slavs of eastern Europe, the Teutons of middle Europe, the English of Great Britain and America, the Romance nations of Southern and Western Europe, the Negroes of Africa and America, the Semitic people of Western Asia and Northern Africa, the Hindoos of Central Asia and the Mongolians of Eastern Asia. There are, of course, other minor race groups, as the American Indians, the Esquimaux and the South Sea Islanders; these larger races, too, are far from homogeneous; the Slav includes the Czech, the Magyar, the Pole and the Russian; the Teuton includes the German, the Scandinavian and the Dutch; the English include the Scotch, the Irish and the conglomerate American. Under Romance nations the widely-differing Frenchman, Italian, Sicilian and Spaniard are comprehended. The term Negro is, perhaps, the most indefinite of all, combining the Mulattoes and Zamboes of America and the Egyptians, Bantus and Bushmen of Africa. Among the Hindoos are traces of widely differing nations, while the great Chinese, Tartar, Corean and Japanese families fall under the one designation—Mongolian.

The question now is: What is the real distinction between these nations? Is it the physical differences of blood, color and cranial measurements? Certainly we must all acknowledge that physical differences play a great part, and that, with wide exceptions and qualifications, these eight great races of to-day follow the cleavage of physical race distinctions. . . . But while race differences have followed mainly physical race lines, yet no mere physical distinctions would really define or explain the deeper differences—the cohesiveness and continuity of these groups. The deeper differences are spiritual, psychical, differences—undoubtedly based on the physical, but infinitely transcending them. . . .

What shall be the function [of race differences] in the future? Manifestly some of the great races of today—particularly the Negro race—have not as yet given to civilization the full spiritual message which they are capable of giving. I will not say that the Negro race has as yet given no message to the world, for it is still a mooted question among scientists as to just how far Egyptian civilization was Negro in its origin; if it was not wholly Negro, it was certainly very closely allied. Be that as it may, however, the fact still remains that the full, complete Negro message of the whole Negro race has not as yet been given to the world. . . . The question is, then: How shall this message be delivered; how shall these various ideals be realized? The answer is plain: By the development of these race groups, not as individuals, but as races. . . . For the development of Negro genius, of Negro literature and art, of Negro spirit, only Negroes bound and welded together, Negroes inspired by one vast ideal, can work out in its fullness the great message we have for humanity. We cannot reverse history; we are subject to the same natural laws as other races, and if the Negro is ever to be a factor in the world's history—if among the gaily-colored banners that deck the broad ramparts of civilization is to hang one uncompromising black, then it must be placed there by black hands, fashioned by black heads and hallowed by the travail of 200,000,000 black hearts beating in one glad song of jubilee.

For this reason, the advance guard of the Negro people—the 8,000,000 people of Negro blood in the United States of America—must soon come to realize that if they are to take their just place in the van of Pan-Negroism, then their destiny is *not* absorption by the white Americans. That if in America it is to be proven for the first time in the modern world that not only Negroes are capable of evolving [great] individual men . . . , but are a nation stored with wonderful possibilities of culture, then their destiny is not a servile imitation of Anglo-Saxon culture, but a stalwart originality which shall unswervingly follow Negro ideals.

It may, however, be objected here that the situation of our race in

America renders this attitude impossible; that our sole hope of salvation lies in our being able to lose our race identity in the commingled blood of the nation; and that any other course would merely increase the friction of races which we call race prejudice, and against which we have so long and so earnestly fought.

Here, then, is the dilemma, and it is a puzzling one, I admit. No Negro who has given earnest thought to the situation of his people in America has failed, at some time in life, to find himself at these cross-roads; has failed to ask himself at some time: What, after all, am I? Am I an American or am I a Negro? Can I be both? Or is it my duty to cease to be a Negro as soon as possible and be an American? If I strive as a Negro, am I not perpetuating the very cleft that threatens and separates Black and White America? Is not my only possible practical aim the subduction of all that is Negro in me to the American? . . .

It is such incessant self-questioning and the hesitation that arises from it, that is making the present period a time of vacillation and contradiction for the American Negro; combined race action is stifled, race responsibility is shirked, race enterprises languish, and the best blood, the best talent, the best energy of the Negro people cannot be marshalled to do the bidding of the race. They stand back to make room for every rascal and demagogue who chooses to cloak his selfish deviltry under the veil of race pride.

Is this right? Is it rational? Is it good policy? Have we in America a distinct mission as a race—a distinct sphere of action and an opportunity for race development, or is self-obliteration the highest end to which Negro blood dare aspire?

If we carefully consider what race prejudice really is, we find it, historically, to be nothing but the friction between different groups of people; it is the difference in aim, in feeling, in ideals of two different races; if, now, this difference exists touching territory, laws, language, or even religion, it is manifest that these people cannot live in the same territory without fatal collision; but if, on the other hand, there is substantial agreement in laws, language and religion; if there is a satisfactory adjustment of economic life, then there is no reason why, in the same country and on the same street, two or three great national ideals might not thrive and develop, that men of different races might not strive together for their race ideals as well, perhaps even better, than in isolation. Here, it seems to me, is the reading of the riddle that puzzles so many of us. We are Americans, not only by birth and by citizenship, but by our political ideals, our language, our religion. Farther than that, our Americanism does not go. At that point, we are Negroes, members of a vast historic race that from the very dawn of creation has slept, but half awakening in the dark forests of its African fatherland. We are the first fruits of this new nation, the harbinger of that black to-morrow which is yet destined to soften the whiteness of the Teutonic to-day. We are that people whose subtle sense of song has given America its only American music, its only American fairy tales, its only touch of pathos and humor amid its mad money-getting plutocracy. As such, it is our duty to conserve our physical powers, our intellectual endowments, our spiritual ideals; as a race we must strive by race organization, by race solidarity, by race unity to the realization of that broader humanity which freely recognizes differences in men, but sternly deprecates inequality in their opportunities of development.

For the accomplishment of these ends we need race organizations: Negro colleges, Negro newspapers, Negro business organizations, a Negro school of literature and art, and an intellectual clearing house, for all these products of the Negro mind. . . . Not only is all this necessary for positive advance, it is absolutely imperative for negative defense. Let us not deceive ourselves at our situation in this country. Weighted with a heritage of moral iniquity from our past history, hard pressed in the economic world by foreign immigrants and native prejudice, hated here, despised there and pitied everywhere; our one haven of refuge is ourselves, and but one means of advance, our own belief in our great destiny, our own implicit trust in our ability and worth. There is no power under God's high heaven that can stop the advance of eight thousand thousand honest, earnest, inspired and united people. But—and here is the rub—they *must* be honest, fearlessly criticising their own faults, zealously correcting them; they must be *earnest*. No people that laughs at itself, and ridicules itself, and wishes to God it was anything but itself ever wrote its name in history; it *must* be inspired with the Divine faith of our black mothers, that out of the blood and dust of battle will march a victorious host, a mighty nation, a peculiar people, to speak to the nations of earth a Divine truth that shall make them free. And such a people must be united; not merely united for the organized theft of political spoils, not united to disgrace religion with whoremongers and ward-heelers; not united merely to protest and pass resolutions, but united to stop the ravages of consumption among the Negro people, united to keep black boys from loafing, gambling and crime; united to guard the purity of black women and to reduce that vast army of black prostitutes that is today marching to hell; and united in serious organizations, to determine by careful conference and thoughtful interchange of opinion the broad lines of policy and action for the American Negro. . . .

Finally, in practical policy, I wish to suggest the following . . . *Creed:*

1. We believe that the Negro people, as a race, have a contribution to make to civilization and humanity, which no other race can make.

2. We believe it the duty of the Americans of Negro descent, as a body, to maintain their race identity until this mission of the Negro people is accomplished, and the ideal of human brotherhood has become a practical possibility.

3. We believe that, unless modern civilization is a failure, it is entirely feasible and practicable for two races in such essential political, economic and religious harmony as the white and colored people of America, to develop side by side in peace and mutual happiness, the peculiar contribution which each has to make to the culture of their common country.

4. As a means to this end we advocate, not such social equality between these races as would disregard human likes and dislikes, but such a social equilibrium as would, throughout all the complicated relations of life, give due and just consideration to culture, ability, and moral worth, whether they be found under white or black skins.

5. We believe that the first and greatest step toward the settlement of the present friction between the races—commonly called the Negro Problem—lies in the correction of the immorality, crime and laziness among the Negroes themselves, which still remains as a heritage from slavery. We believe that only earnest and long continued efforts on our own part can cure these social ills.

6. We believe that the second great step toward a better adjustment of the relations between the races, should be a more impartial selection of ability in the economic and intellectual world, and a greater respect for personal liberty and worth, regardless of race. We believe that only earnest efforts on the part of the white people of this country will bring much needed reform in these matters.

7. On the basis of the foregoing declaration, and firmly believing in our high destiny, we, as American Negroes, are resolved to strive in every honorable way for the realization of the best and highest aims, for the development of strong manhood and pure womanhood,

and for the rearing of a race ideal in America and Africa, to the glory of God and the uplifting of the Negro people.

THE "TALENTED TENTH" [3]

The Negro race, like all races, is going to be saved by its exceptional men. The problem of education, then, among Negroes must first of all deal with the Talented Tenth; it is the problem of developing the Best of this race that they may guide the Mass away from the contamination and death of the Worst, in their own and other races. Now the training of men is a difficult and intricate task. Its technique is a matter for educational experts, but its object is for the vision of seers. If we make money the object of man-training, we shall develop money-makers but not necessarily men; if we make technical skill the object of education, we may possess artisans but not, in nature, men. Men we shall have only as we make manhood the object of the work of the schools—intelligence, broad sympathy, knowledge of the world that was and is, and of the relation of men to it—this is the curriculum of that Higher Education which must underlie true life. On this foundation we may build bread winning, skill of hand and quickness of brain, with never a fear lest the child and man mistake the means of living for the object of life.

If this be true—and who can deny it—three tasks lay before me; first to show from the past that the Talented Tenth as they have risen among American Negroes have been worthy of leadership; secondly, to show how these men may be educated and developed; and thirdly, to show their relation to the Negro problem.

From the very first it has been the educated and intelligent of the Negro people that have led and elevated the mass, and the sole obstacles that nullified and retarded their efforts were slavery and race prejudice. . . .

And so we come to the present—a day of cowardice and vacillation, of strident wide-voiced wrong and faint hearted compromise; of double-faced dallying with Truth and Right. Who are to-day guiding the work of the Negro people? The "exceptions" of course. And yet so sure as this Talented Tenth is pointed out, the blind

[3] "The Talented Tenth," in Booker T. Washington *et al., The Negro Problem: A Series of Articles by Representative American Negroes of To-Day* (New York: James Pott & Co., 1903), pp. 33–75.

worshippers of the Average cry out in alarm: "These are exceptions, look here at death, disease and crime—these are the happy rule." Of course they are the rule, because a silly nation made them the rule: Because for three long centuries this people lynched Negroes who dared to be brave, raped black women who dared to be virtuous, crushed dark-hued youth who dared to be ambitious, and encouraged and made to flourish servility and lewdness and apathy. But not even this was able to crush all manhood and chastity and aspiration from black folk. A saving remnant continually survives and persists, continually aspires, continually shows itself in thrift and ability and character. Exceptional it is to be sure, but this is its chiefest promise; it shows the capability of Negro blood, the promise of black men. . . . Is it fair, is it decent, is it Christian to ignore these facts of the Negro problem, to belittle such aspiration, to nullify such leadership and seek to crush these people back into the mass out of which by toil and travail, they and their fathers have raised themselves?

Can the masses of the Negro people be in any possible way more quickly raised than by the effort and example of this aristocracy of talent and character? Was there ever a nation on God's fair earth civilized from the bottom upward? Never; it is, ever was and ever will be from the top downward that culture filters. The Talented Tenth rises and pulls all that are worth the saving up to their vantage ground. This is the history of human progress. . . .

How then shall the leaders of a struggling people be trained and the hands of the risen few strengthened? There can be but one answer: The best and most capable of their youth must be schooled in the colleges and universities of the land. . . .

All men cannot go to college but some men must; every isolated group or nation must have its yeast, must have for the talented few centers of training where men are not so mystified and befuddled by the hard and necessary toil of earning a living, as to have no aims higher than their bellies, and no God greater than Gold. This is true training. . . .

The main question, so far as the Southern Negro is concerned, is: What under the present circumstance, must a system of education do in order to raise the Negro as quickly as possible in the scale of civilization? The answer to this question seems to me clear: It must strengthen the Negro's character, increase his knowledge and teach him to earn a living. Now it goes without saying, that it is hard to do all these things simultaneously or suddenly, and that at the same time it will not do to give all the attention to one and neglect the others; we could give black boys trades, but that alone will not civilize a race of ex-slaves; we might simply increase their knowledge of the world, but this would not necessarily make them wish to use this knowledge honestly; we might seek to strengthen character and purpose, but to what end if this people have nothing to eat or to wear? . . . If then we start out to train an ignorant and unskilled people with a heritage of bad habits, our system of training must set before itself two great aims—the one dealing with knowledge and character, the other part seeking to give the child the technical knowledge necessary for him to earn a living under the present circumstances. These objects are accomplished in part by the opening of the common schools on the one, and of the industrial schools on the other. But only in part, for there must also be trained those who are to teach these schools—men and women of knowledge and culture and technical skill who understand modern civilization, and have the training and aptitude to impart it to the children under them. There must be teachers, and teachers of teachers, and to attempt to establish any sort of a system of common and industrial school training, without *first* (and I say *first* advisedly) without *first* providing for the higher training of the very best teachers, is simply throwing your money to the winds. . . . Nothing, in these latter days, has so dampened the faith of thinking Negroes in recent educational movements, as the fact that such movements have been accompanied by ridicule and denouncement and decrying of those very institutions of higher training which made the Negro public school possible, and make Negro industrial schools thinkable. . . .

I would not deny, or for a moment seem to deny, the paramount necessity of teaching the Negro to work, and to work steadily and skillfully; or seem to depreciate in the slightest degree the important part industrial schools must play in the accomplishment of these ends, but I *do* say, and insist upon it, that it is industrialism drunk with its vision of success, to imagine that its own work can be accomplished without providing for the training of broadly cultured men and women to teach its own teachers, and to teach the teachers of the public schools. . . .

I am an earnest advocate of manual training and trade teaching for black boys, and for white boys, too. I believe that next to the founding of Negro colleges the most valuable addition to Negro education since the war, has been industrial training for black boys. Nevertheless, I insist that the object of all true education is not to make men carpenters, it is to make carpenters men; there are two means of making the carpenter a man, each equally important: the first is to give the group and community in which he works, liberally trained teachers and leaders to teach him and his family what life means; the second is to give him sufficient intelligence and technical skill to make him an efficient workman; the first object demands the Negro college and college-bred men—not a quantity of such colleges, but a few of excellent quality; not too many college-bred men, but enough to leaven the lump, to inspire the masses, to raise the Talented Tenth to leadership; the second object demands a good system of common schools, well-taught, conveniently located and properly equipped. . . .

Thus, again, in the manning of trade schools and manual training schools we are thrown back upon the higher training as its source and chief support. There was a time when any aged and wornout carpenter could teach in a trade school. But not so to-day. Indeed the demand for college-bred men by a school like Tuskegee, ought to make Mr. Booker T. Washington the firmest friend of higher training. . . . And yet one of the effects of Mr. Washington's propaganda has been to throw doubt upon the expediency of such training for Negroes. . . .

Men of America, the problem is plain before you. Here is a race transplanted through the criminal foolishness of your fathers. Whether you like it or not the millions are here, and here they will remain. If you do not lift them up, they will pull you down. Education and work are the levers to uplift a people. Work alone will not do it unless inspired by the right ideals and guided by intelligence. Education must not simply teach work—it must teach Life. The Talented Tenth of the Negro race must be made leaders of thought and missionaries of culture among their people. No others can do this work and Negro colleges must train men for it. The Negro race, like all other races, is going to be saved by its exceptional men.

DU BOIS' "PARTING OF THE WAYS" WITH BOOKER T. WASHINGTON [4]

. . . Yet the plain result of the attitude of mind of those who, in their advocacy of industrial schools, the unimportance of suffrage and civil rights and conciliation, have been significantly silent or evasive as to higher training and the great principle of free self-

[4] "The Parting of the Ways," in "The Negro Problem from the Negro Point of View," *The World Today*, VI (April 1904), 521–23.

respecting manhood for black folk—the plain result of this propaganda has been to help the cutting down of educational opportunity for Negro children, the legal disfranchisement of nearly 5,000,000 of Negroes and a state of public opinion which apologizes for lynching, listens complacently to any insult or detraction directed against an eighth of the population of the land, and silently allows a new slavery to rise and clutch the South and paralyze the moral sense of a great nation.

What do Negroes say to this? I speak advisedly when I say that the overwhelming majority of them declare that the tendencies to-day are wrong and that the propaganda that encouraged them was wrong. They say that industrial and trade teaching is needed among Negroes, sadly needed; but they unhesitatingly affirm that it is not needed as much as thorough common school training and the careful education of the gifted in higher institutions; that only in this way can a people rise by intelligence and social leadership to a plane of permanent efficiency and morality.

Moreover, . . . black men in this land know that when they lose the ballot they lose all. They are no fools. They know it is impossible for free workingmen without a ballot to compete with free workingmen who have the ballot; they know there is no set of people so good and true as to be worth trusting with the political destiny of their fellows, and they know that it is just as true to-day as it was a century and a quarter ago that "Taxation without representation is tyranny."

Finally, the Negro knows perfectly what freedom and equality mean—opportunity to make the best of oneself, unhandicapped by wanton restraint and unreasoning prejudice. For this the most of us propose to strive. We will not, by word or deed, for a moment admit the right of any man to discriminate against us simply on account of race or color. Whenever we submit to humiliation and oppression it is because of superior brute force; and even when bending to the inevitable we bend with unabated protest and declare flatly and unswervingly that any man or section or nation who wantonly shuts the doors of opportunity and self-defense in the faces of the weak is a coward and knave. We refuse to kiss the hands that smite us, but rather insist on striving by all civilized methods to keep wide educational opportunity, to keep the right to vote, to insist on equal civil rights and to gain every right and privilege open to a free American citizen.

But, answer some, you can not accomplish this. America will never spell opportunity for black men; it spelled slavery for them in 1619 and it will spell the same thing in other letters in 1919. To this I answer simply: I do not believe it. I believe that black men will become free American citizens if they have the courage and persistence to demand the rights and treatment of men, and cease to toady and apologize and belittle themselves. The rights of humanity are worth fighting for. Those that deserve them in the long run get them. The way for black men to-day to make these rights the heritage of their children is to struggle for them unceasingly, and if they fail, die trying.

DU BOIS' "CREDO" 5

I believe in God who made of one blood all races that dwell on earth.

I believe that all men, black and brown and white, are brothers, varying, through Time and Opportunity, in form and gift and feature, but differing in no essential particular, and alike in soul and in the possibility of infinite development.

Especially do I believe in the Negro Race; in the beauty of its genius, the sweetness of its soul, and its strength in that meekness which shall yet inherit this turbulent earth.

I believe in pride of race and lineage and self; in pride of self so deep as to scorn injustice to other selves; in pride of lineage so great as to despise no man's father; in pride of race so chivalrous as neither to offer bastardy to the weak nor beg wedlock of the strong, knowing that men may be brothers in Christ, even tho they be not brothers-in-law.

I believe in Service—humble reverent service, from the blackening of boots to the whitening of souls; for Work is Heaven, Idleness Hell, and Wage is the "Well done!" of the Master who summoned all them that labor and are heavy laden, making no distinction between the black sweating cotton-hands of Georgia and the First Families of Virginia, since all distinction not based on deed is devilish and not divine.

I believe in the Devil and his angels, who wantonly work to narrow the opportunity of struggling human beings, especially if they be black; who spit in the faces of the fallen, strike them that cannot

---

5 "Credo," *The Independent*, LVII (October 6, 1904), 787.

strike again, believe the worst and work to prove it, hating the image which their Maker stamped on a brother's soul.

I believe in the Prince of Peace. I believe that War is Murder. I believe that armies and navies are at bottom the tinsel and braggadocio of oppression and wrong; and I believe that the wicked conquest of weaker and darker nations by nations whiter and stronger but foreshadows the death of that strength.

I believe in Liberty for all men; the space to stretch their arms and their souls; the right to breathe and the right to vote, the freedom to choose their friends, enjoy the sunshine and ride on the railroads, uncursed by color; thinking, dreaming, working as they will in a kingdom of God and love.

I believe in the training of children black even as white; the leading out of little souls into the green pastures and beside the still waters, not for pelf or peace, but for Life lit by some large vision of beauty and goodness and truth; lest we forget, and the sons of the fathers, like Esau, for mere meat barter their birthright in a mighty nation.

Finally, I believe in Patience—patience with the weakness of the Weak and the strength of the Strong, the prejudice of the Ignorant and the ignorance of the Blind; patience with the tardy triumph of Joy and the mad chastening of Sorrow—patience with God.

"THE SOULS OF WHITE FOLK" [6]

. . . Unfortunate? Unfortunate. But where is the misfortune? Mine? Am I in my blackness the sole sufferer? I suffer. And yet, somehow, above the suffering, above the shackled anger that beats the bars, above the hurt that crazes, surges in me a vast pity—pity for a people prisoned and enthralled, hampered and made miserable for such a cause, for such a fantasy.

I sit and see the souls of the White Folk daily shriveling and dying in the fierce flame of this new fanaticism. Whither has gone America's proud moral leadership of the world? Where is the generous thought, the sweet applause, the soul's wide freedom with which we once were wont to greet the up-struggling of human kind? . . .

Onward we reel. Peace? Ten thousand dollars for peace and two

[6] "The Souls of White Folk," *The Independent*, LXIX (August 18, 1910), 339–42.

hundred millions for war. How can there be peace for those who
are white and hate "niggers"? Democracy? Absurd! Dream of infants!
Let Disfranchisement and Privilege and a Solid South rule this great
republic. The rights of woman? Are not American women the best
dressed in the world? Do they not bring the highest titles in the
market? Does free America want to enfranchise any more dagoes
and hybrids?

It is not alone this pitiful striking of colors in the great world
crusade for liberty, equality and brotherhood; it is the humiliating
thought in our own souls that this outward surrender is the honest
counterpart of the inward degeneration—the deliberate crippling
and deforming of the Souls of White Folk by the glorification of
Color Caste.

To you this is less immediately apparent than to me; for before me
the Souls of White Folk stand singularly naked. In my presence they
tend to lay aside all their little lies and hypocrisies and bathe in
brutal frankness. Why not? Am I a millionaire? Have I a political
pull? Have I social prestige? Have I any brains? I bear the shadowed
answer on my face. Well, then, be thrifty. Why waste manners,
beauty, courtesy or conversation on me? There's nought to gain and
much to lose, for the watchful world is sitting near ready to resent
social equality. Therefore, he who seems to you a gentleman is but
his boorish self to me; she who is to you a vision of womanly loveliness may be but selfish vulgarity to me. Such nastier aspects of
modern American life flash repeatedly both on me and mine, so
that I realize even more vividly than you how thoroughly and persistently we are making these things characteristic of the nation, the
measure of its thought and soul, every time you make the measure
of a man, whiteness. Why not? There is no logical escape. A true
and worthy ideal frees and uplifts a people; a false ideal imprisons
and lowers. Say to men, earnestly and repeatedly: "Honesty is best;
knowledge is power; do unto others as you would be done by." Say
this and act it, and the nation must move toward it if not to it. But
say to a people: "The one virtue is to be white," and the people
rush to the one inevitable conclusion, "Kill the 'nigger'!"

Is not this the record of present America? Is not this its headlong
progress? Are we not coming more and more day by day to making
the statement, "I am white," the one fundamental tenet of our
practical morality? Only when this basic iron rule is involved is
our defense of right nationwide prompt. Murder may swagger, theft
may rule and prostitution flourish, and the nation gives but spas-

modic, intermittent and lukewarm attention. But let the murderer be black or the thief brown or the violator of womanhood have but a drop of negro blood, and the righteousness of the indignation sweeps the world. Nor would this fact make the indignation less justifiable did not we all know that it was blackness that was condemned, and not crime. . . .

ON RACE PRIDE [7]

Any colored man who complains of the treatment he receives in America is apt to be faced sooner or later by the statement that he is ashamed of his race.

The statement usually strikes him as a most astounding piece of illogical reasoning, to which a hot reply is appropriate.

And yet notice the curious logic of the persons who say such things. They argue:

White men alone are men. This Negro wants to be a man. *Ergo* he wants to be a white man.

Their attention is drawn to the efforts of colored people to be treated decently. This minor premise there attracts them. But the major premise—the question as to treating black men like white men—never enters their heads, nor can they conceive it entering the black man's head. If he wants to be a man he must want to be white, and therefore it is with peculiar complacency that a Tennessee paper says of a dark champion of Negro equality: "He bitterly resents his Negro blood."

Not so, O Blind Man. He bitterly resents your treatment of Negro blood. The prouder he is, or has a right to be, of the blood of his black fathers, the more doggedly he resists the attempt to load men of that blood with ignominy and chains. It is race pride that fights for freedom; it is the man ashamed of his blood who weakly submits and smiles.

A PROGRAM OF ACTION FOR BLACK AMERICA [8]

The immediate program of the American Negro means nothing unless it is mediate to his great ideal and the ultimate ends of his development. We need not waste time by seeking to deceive

[7] "Ashamed," *The Crisis,* I (January 1911), 21.
[8] "The Immediate Program of the American Negro," *The Crisis,* IX (April 1915), 310–12.

our enemies into thinking that we are going to be content with a half loaf, or by being willing to lull our friends into a false sense of our indifference and present satisfaction.

The American Negro demands equality—political equality, industrial equality and social equality; and he is never going to rest satisfied with anything less. He demands this in no spirit of braggadocio and with no obsequious envy of others, but as an absolute measure of self-defense and the only one that will assure to the darker races their ultimate survival on earth.

Only in a demand and a persistent demand for essential equality in the modern realm of human culture can any people show a real pride of race and a decent self-respect. For any group, nation or race to admit for a moment the present monstrous demand of the white race to be the inheritors of the earth, the arbiters of mankind and the sole owners of a heritage of culture which they did not create, nor even improve to any greater extent than the other great division of men—to admit such pretense for a moment is for the race to write itself down immediately as indisputably inferior in judgment, knowledge and common sense. . . .

The Negro must have political freedom; taxation without representation is tyranny. American Negroes of to-day are ruled by tyrants who take what they please in taxes and give what they please in law and administration, in justice and in injustice; and the great mass of black people must stand helpless and voiceless before a condition which has time and time again caused other peoples to fight and die.

The Negro must have industrial freedom. Between the peonage of the rural South, the oppression of shrewd capitalists and the jealousy of certain trade unions, the Negro laborer is the most exploited class in the country, giving more hard toil for less money than any other American, and have less voice in the conditions of his labor.

In social intercourse every effort is being made to-day from the President of the United States and the so-called Church of Christ down to saloons and boot-blacks to segregate, strangle and spiritually starve Negroes so as to give them the least possible chance to know and share civilization.

These shackles must go. But that is but the beginning. The Negro must have power; the power of men, the right to do, to know, to feel and to express that knowledge, action and spiritual gift. He must not simply be free from the political tyranny of white folk, he must have the right to vote and to rule over the citizens, white and black, to the extent of his proven foresight and ability. He must have a voice in the new industrial democracy which is building and the power to see to it that his children are not in the next generation trained to be the mudsills of society. He must have the right to social intercourse with his fellows. . . .

What now are the practical steps which must be taken to accomplish these ends?

First of all before taking steps the wise man knows the object and end of his journey. There are those who would advise the black man to pay little or no attention to where he is going so long as he keeps moving. They assume that God or his vice-regent the White Man will attend to the steering. This is arrant nonsense. The feet of those that aimlessly wander land as often in hell as in heaven. Conscious self-realization and self-direction is the watchword of modern man, and the first article in the program of any group that will survive must be the great aim, equality and power among men.

The practical steps to this are clear. *First* we must fight obstructions; by continual and increasing effort we must first make American courts either build up a body of decisions which will protect the plain legal rights of American citizens or else make them tear down the civil and political rights of all citizens in order to oppress a few. . . .

We must *secondly* seek in legislature and congress remedial legislation; national aid to public school education, the removal of all legal discriminations based simply on race and color, and those marriage laws passed to make the seduction of black girls easy and without legal penalty.

Third the human contact of human beings must be increased; the policy which brings into sympathetic touch and understanding, men and women, rich and poor, capitalist and laborer, Asiatic and European, must bring into closer contact and mutual knowledge the white and black people of this land. It is the most frightful indictment of a country which dares to call itself civilized that it has allowed itself to drift into a state of ignorance where ten million people are coming to believe that all white people are liars and thieves, and the whites in turn to believe that the chief industry of Negroes is raping white women.

Fourth only the publication of the truth repeatedly and incisively and uncompromisingly can secure that change in public opinion which will correct these awful lies. . . .

Such is the program of work against obstructions. Let us now turn to constructive effort. This may be summed up under (1) economic co-operation (2) a revival of art and literature (3) political action (4) education and (5) organization.

Under economic co-operation we must strive to spread the idea among colored people that the accumulation of wealth is for social rather than individual ends. We must avoid, in the advancement of the Negro race, the mistakes of ruthless exploitation which have marked modern economic history. To this end we must seek not simply home ownership, small landholding and saving accounts, but also all forms of co-operation, both in production and distribution, profit sharing, building and loan associations, systematic charity for definite, practical ends, systematic migration from mob rule and robbery, to freedom and enfranchisement, the emancipation of women and the abolition of child labor.

In art and literature we should try to loose the tremendous emotional wealth of the Negro and the dramatic strength of his problems through writing, the stage, pageantry and other forms of art. We should resurrect forgotten ancient Negro art and history, and we should set the black man before the world as both a creative artist and a strong subject for artistic treatment.

In political action we should organize the votes of Negroes in such congressional districts as have any number of Negro voters. We should systematically interrogate candidates on matters vital to Negro freedom and uplift. We should train colored voters to reject the bribe of office and to accept only decent legal enactments both for their own uplift and for the uplift of laboring classes of all races and both sexes.

In education we must seek to give colored children free public school training. We must watch with grave suspicion the attempt of those who, under the guise of vocational training, would fasten ignorance and menial service on the Negro for another generation. . . .

It is our duty then, not drastically but persistently, to seek out colored children of ability and genius, to open up to them broader, industrial opportunity and above all, to find that Talented Tenth and encourage it by the best and most exhaustive training in order to supply the Negro race and the world with leaders, thinkers and artists.

For the accomplishment of all these ends we must organize. Organization among us already has gone far but it must go much further and higher. Organization is sacrifice. It is sacrifice of opinions, of time, of work and of money, but it is, after all, the cheapest way of buying the most priceless of gifts—freedom and efficiency. . . .

2
On Art for Its Sake and as Propaganda

Du Bois gained much critical recognition as a writer of prose. Writing in 1907, for example, Henry James asked: "How can everything so have gone that the only 'Southern' book of any distinction published for many a year is The Souls of Black Folk, *by that most accomplished of members of the negro race, Mr. W. E. B. Du Bois?" Twenty years later America's most noted playwright, Eugene O'Neill, also praised Du Bois as a writer. "Ranking as he does among the foremost writers of true importance in the country," O'Neill wrote, "one sometimes wishes . . . that he could devote all of his time to the accomplishment of that fine and moving prose which distinguishes his books. But at the same time one realizes . . . that with Dr. Du Bois it is a cause—an ideal— that overcomes the personal egoism of the artist." This ideal —full personhood for America's blacks—frequently injected itself into his writings. As a cultural nationalist, Du Bois urged Afro-Americans to "train ourselves to see beauty in blackness." Du Bois also argued that blacks, being an oppressed minority, had a unique perspective on America. "We who are dark," he wrote, "can see America in a way that white Americans cannot." Anti-white bitterness as well as black pride was evident in much of Du Bois' prose and poetry, which, he frankly contended, were works not only of art but also of propaganda. "I stand in utter shamelessness," he acknowledged in 1926, "and say that whatever art I have for writing has been used always for propaganda for gaining the right of black people to love and enjoy."*

". . . LET US TRAIN OURSELVES TO SEE BEAUTY IN BLACK"[1]

It was in Chicago. John Haynes Holmes was talking.
He said: "I met two children—one as fair as the dawn—the

[1] "In Black," *The Crisis*, XX (October 1920), 263, 266.

other as beautiful as the night." Then he paused. He had to pause for the audience guffawed in wild merriment. Why?

It was a colored audience. Many of them were black. Some black faces there were as beautiful as the night.

Why did they laugh?

Because the world had taught them to be ashamed of their color.

Because for 500 years men had hated and despised and abused black folk.

And now in strange, inexplicable transposition the rising blacks laugh at themselves in nervous, blatant, furtive merriment.

They laugh because they think they are expected to laugh— because all their poor hunted lives they have heard "black" things laughed at.

Of all the pitiful things of this pitiful race problem, this is the pitifullest. So curious a mental state tends to further subtleties. Colored folk, like all folk, love to see themselves in pictures; but they are afraid to see the types which the white world has carica- tured. The whites obviously seldom picture brown and yellow folk, but for five centuries they have exhausted every ingenuity of trick, of ridicule and caricature on black folk: "grinning" Negroes, "happy" Negroes, "gold dust twins," "Aunt Jemimas," "solid" headed tacks—everything and anything to make Negroes ridicu- lous. . . .

It is not that we are ashamed of our color and blood. We are instinctively and almost unconsciously ashamed of the caricatures done of our darker shades. Black *is* caricature in our half conscious thought and we shun in print and paint that which we love in life. How good a dark face looks to us in a strange white city! How the black soldiers, despite their white French sweethearts, yearned for their far-off "brown-skins." A mighty and swelling human con- sciousness is leading us joyously to embrace the darker world, but we remain afraid of black pictures because they are the cruel re- minders of the crimes of Sunday "comics" and "Nigger" minstrels.

Off with these thought-chains and inchoate soul-shrinkings, and let us train ourselves to see beauty in black.

ART AS PROPAGANDA[2]

. . . What do we want? What is the thing we are after? . . . We want to be Americans, full-fledged Americans, with all the

[2] "Criteria of Negro Art," *The Crisis,* XXXII (October 1926), 290–97.

rights of other American citizens. But is that all? Do we want simply to be Americans? Once in a while through all of us there flashes some clairvoyance, some clear idea, of what America really is. We who are dark can see America in a way that white Americans can not. And seeing our country thus, are we satisfied with its present goals and ideals? . . .

Thus it is the bounden duty of black America to begin this great work of the creation of Beauty, of the preservation of Beauty, of the realization of Beauty, and we must use in this work all the methods that men have used before. And what have been the tools of the artist in times gone by? First of all, he has used the Truth— not for the sake of truth, not as a scientist seeking truth, but as one upon whom Truth eternally thrusts itself as the highest hand-maid of imagination, as the one great vehicle of universal under-standing. Again artists have used Goodness—goodness in all its aspects of justice, honor and right—not for sake of an ethical sanc-tion but as the one true method of gaining sympathy and human interest.

The apostle of Beauty thus becomes the apostle of Truth and Right not by choice but by inner and outer compulsion. Free he is but his freedom is ever bounded by Truth and Justice; and slavery only dogs him when he is denied the right to tell the Truth or recognize an ideal of Justice.

Thus all Art is propaganda and ever must be, despite the wailing of the purists. I stand in utter shamelessness and say that whatever art I have for writing has been used always for propaganda for gaining the right of black folk to love and enjoy. I do not care a damn for any art that is not used for propaganda. But I do care when propaganda is confined to one side while the other is stripped and silent. . . .

A POEM COMMEMORATING WHITE LAWLESSNESS AND BLACK DESPAIR DURING THE ATLANTA RACE RIOT OF 1906 [3]

O Silent God, Thou whose voice afar in mist and mystery hath left our ears an-hungered in these fearful days—
   Hear us, good Lord!
Listen to us, Thy children: our faces dark with doubt are made a mockery in Thy Sanctuary. With uplifted hands we front Thy Heaven, O God, crying:

[3] "A Litany of Atlanta," *The Independent*, LXI (October 11, 1906), 856–58.

We beseech Thee to hear us, good Lord!

We are not better than our fellows, Lord; we are but weak and human men. When our devils do deviltry, curse Thou the doer and the deed,—curse them as we curse them, do to them all and more than ever they have done to innocence and weakness, to womanhood and home.

Have mercy upon us, miserable sinners!

And yet, whose is the deeper guilt? Who made these devils? Who nursed them in crime and fed them on injustice? Who ravished and debauched their mothers and their grandmothers? Who bought and sold their crime and waxed fat and rich on public iniquity?

Thou knowest, good God!

Is this Thy Justice, O Father, that guile be easier than innocence and the innocent be crucified for the guilt of the untouched guilty?

Justice, O Judge of men!

Wherefore do we pray? Is not the God of the Fathers dead? Have not seers seen in Heaven's halls Thine hearsed and lifeless form stark amidst the black and rolling smoke of sin, where all along bow bitter forms of endless dead?

Awake, Thou that sleepest!

Thou art not dead, but flown afar, up hills of endless light, through blazing corridors of suns, where worlds do swing of good and gentle men, of women strong and free—far from the cozenage, black hypocrisy, and chaste prostitution of this shameful speck of dust!

Turn again, O Lord; leave us not to perish in our sin!

From lust of body and lust of blood,—

Great God, deliver us!

From lust of power and lust of gold,—

Great God, deliver us!

From the leagued lying of despot and of brute,—

Great God, deliver us!

A city lay in travail, God our Lord, and from her loins sprang twin Murder and Black Hate. Red was the midnight; clang, crack, and cry of death and fury filled the air and trembled underneath the stars where church spires pointed silently to Thee. And all this was to sate the greed of greedy men who hide behind the veil of vengeance!

Bend us Thine ear, O Lord!

In the pale, still morning we looked upon the deed. We stopped our ears and held our leaping hands, but they—did they not wag

their heads and leer and cry with bloody jaws: *Cease from Crime!*
The word was mockery, for thus they train a hundred crimes while
we do cure one.

   Turn again our captivity, O Lord!

Behold this maimed and broken thing, dear God; it was an
humble black man, who toiled and sweat to save a bit from the
pittance paid him. They told him: *Work and Rise!* He worked. Did
this man sin? Nay, but someone told how someone said another
did—one whom he had never seen nor known. Yet for that man's
crime this man lieth maimed and murdered, his wife naked to
shame, his children to poverty and evil.

   Hear us, O heavenly Father!

Doth not this justice of hell stink in Thy nostrils, O God? How
long shall the mounting flood of innocent blood roar in Thine
ears and pound in our hearts for vengeance? Pile the pale frenzy
of blood-crazed brutes, who do such deeds, high on Thine Altar,
Jehovah Jireh, and burn it in hell forever and forever!

   Forgive us, good Lord; we know not what we say!

Bewildered we are and passion-tossed, mad with the madness of
a mobbed and mocked and murdered people; straining at the arm-
posts of Thy throne, we raise our shackled hands and charge Thee,
God, by the bones of our stolen fathers, by the tears of our dead
mothers, by the very blood of Thy crucified Christ: What meaneth
this? Tell us the plan; give us the sign!

   Keep not Thou silent, O God!

Sit not longer blind, Lord God, deaf to our prayer and dumb to
our dumb suffering. Surely Thou, too, art not white, O Lord, a
pale, bloodless, heartless thing!

   Ah! Christ of all the Pities!

Forgive the thought! Forgive these wild, blasphemous words!
Thou art still the God of our black fathers and in Thy Soul's Soul
sit some soft darkenings of the evening, some shadowings of the
velvet night.

But whisper—speak—call, great God, for Thy silence is white
terror to our hearts! The way, O God, show us the way and point
us the path!

Whither? North is greed and South is blood; within, the coward,
and without, the liar. Whither? To death?

   Amen! Welcome, dark sleep!

Whither? To life? But not this life, dear God, not this. Let the cup pass from us, tempt us not beyond our strength, for there is that clamoring and clawing within, to whose voice we would not listen, yet shudder lest we must,—and it is red. Ah! God! It is a red and awful shape.

Selah!

In yonder East trembles a star.

Vengeance is Mine; I will repay, saith the Lord!

Thy Will, O Lord, be done!

Kyrie Eleison!

Lord, we have done these pleading, wavering words.

We beseech Thee to hear us, good Lord!

We bow our heads and hearken soft to the sobbing of women and little children.

We beseech Thee to hear us, good Lord!

Our voices sink in silence and in night.

Hear us, good Lord!

In night, O God of a godless land!

Amen!

In silence, O Silent God.

Selah!

"THE SONG OF THE SMOKE"[4]

I am the Smoke King
I am black!
I am swinging in the sky,
I am wringing worlds awry;
I am the thought of the throbbing mills,
I am the soul of the soul-toil kills,
Wraith of the ripple of trading rills;
Up I'm curling from the sod,
I am whirling home to God;
I am the Smoke King
I am black.

I am the Smoke King,
I am black!
I am wreathing broken hearts,
I am sheathing love's light darts;
Inspiration of iron times
Wedding the toil of toiling climes,

[4] "The Song of the Smoke," *The Horizon,* I (February 1907), 4–6.

Shedding the blood of bloodless crimes—
Lurid lowering 'mid the blue,
Torrid towering toward the true,
    I am the Smoke King,
    I am black.

    I am the Smoke King,
    I am black!
I am darkening with song,
I am hearkening to wrong!
    I will be black as blackness can—
    The blacker the mantle, the mightier the man!
    For blackness was ancient ere whiteness began.
I am daubing God in night,
I am swabbing Hell in white:
    I am the Smoke King
    I am black.

    I am the Smoke King
    I am black!
I am cursing ruddy morn,
I am hearsing hearts unborn:
    Souls unto me are as stars in a night,
    I whiten my black men—I blacken my white!
    What's the hue of a hide to a man in his might?
Hail! great, gritty, grimy hands—
Sweet Christ, pity toiling lands!
    I am the Smoke King
    I am black.

"THE BURDEN OF BLACK WOMEN" [5]

Dark daughter of the lotus leaves that watch the Southern sea,
Wan spirit of a prisoned soul a-panting to be free;
    The muttered music of thy streams, the whispers of the deep
    Have kissed each other in God's name and kissed a world to sleep.

The will of the world is a whistling wind sweeping a cloud-cast sky,
And not from the east and not from the west knelled its soul-searing
    cry;
    But out of the past of the Past's grey past, it yelled from the top of
    the sky;

[5] "The Burden of Black Women," *The Crisis*, IX (November 1914), 31. Also
published in *The Horizon*, II (November 1907), 3–5.

Crying: Awake, O ancient race! Wailing: O woman arise!
And crying and sighing and crying again as a voice in the midnight
   cries;
But the burden of white men bore her back, and the white world
   stifled her sighs.

The White World's vermin and filth:
   All the dirt of London,
   All the scum of New York;
   Valiant spoilers of women
   And conquerors of unarmed men;
   Shameless breeders of bastards
   Drunk with the greed of gold,
   Baiting their blood-stained hooks
   With cant for the souls of the simple,
   Bearing the White Man's Burden
   Of Liquor and Lust and Lies!
   Unthankful we wince in the East,
   Unthankful we wail from the westward,
   Unthankfully thankful we sing,
   In the un-won wastes of the wild:
         I hate them, Oh!
         I hate them well,
         I hate them, Christ!
         As I hate Hell,
         If I were God
         I'd sound their knell
         This day!

Who raised the fools to their glory
But black men of Egypt and Ind?
Ethiopia's sons of the evening,
Chaldeans and Yellow Chinese?
The Hebrew children of Morning
And mongrels of Rome and Greece?
         Ah, well!

And they that raised the boasters
Shall drag them down again:
Down with the theft of their thieving
And murder and mocking of men,
Down with their barter of women
And laying and lying of creeds,

Down with their cheating of childhood,
And drunken orgies of war—

    down,

       down,

          deep down,

Till the Devil's strength be shorn,
Till some dim, darker David a-hoeing of his corn,
And married maiden, Mother of God,
Bid the Black Christ be born!

Then shall the burden of manhood,
Be it yellow or black or white,
And Poverty, Justice and Sorrow—
The Humble and Simple and Strong,
Shall sing with the Sons of Morning
And Daughters of Evensong:

Black mother of the iron hills that guard the blazing sea,
Wild spirit of a storm-swept soul a-struggling to be free,
Where 'neath the bloody finger marks, thy riven bosom quakes,
Thicken the thunders of God's voice, and lo! a world awakes!

ON THE OBSEQUIOUSNESS OF BOOKER T. WASHINGTON, "THE BLACK LEADER" [6]

The White Man looked contemptuously down upon the
Black Leader who smiled back affably. "Get out of here," yelled
the White Man as he kicked the Black Leader down stairs and
tossed a quarter after him. The Black Leader pirouetted and
bumped and rolled until he landed sprawling in the dirt. The
dark and watching crowd were breathless, and one of them grasped
his club and bared his arm. Slowly the Black Leader arose and his
Eager Supporter assiduously brushed off his pants. Then the Black
Leader squared his shoulders and looked about him. He cleared
his throat and the throng hung upon his word breathless, eager,
while the one man clutched his club tighter.

[6] "Constructive Work," *The Horizon*, V (December 1909), 2.

"My friends," said the Black Leader, "the world demands constructive work: it dislikes pessimists. I want to call your attention to the fact that this White gem'man—I mean gentleman—did *not* kick me nearly as hard as he might have: again he wore soft kid boots, and finally I landed in the dirt and not on the asphalt. Moreover," continued the Black Leader as he stooped in the dust, "I am twenty-five cents in." And he walked thoughtfully away, amid the frantic plaudits of the crowd. Except one man. He dropped his club and whispered;

> *"My God!"*

"ON BEING CRAZY" [7]

It was one o'clock and I was hungry. I walked into a restaurant, seated myself and reached for the bill-of-fare. My table companion rose.

"Sir," said he, "do you wish to force your company on those who do not want you?"

No, said I, I wish to eat.

"Are you aware, Sir, that this is social equality?"

Nothing of the sort, Sir, it is hunger,—and I ate.

The day's work done, I sought the theatre. As I sank into my seat, the lady shrank and squirmed.

I beg pardon, I said.

"Do you enjoy being where you are not wanted?" she asked coldly.

Oh no, I said.

"Well you are not wanted here."

I was surprised. I fear you are mistaken, I said. I certainly want the music and I like to think the music wants me to listen to it.

"Usher," said the lady, "this is social equality."

No, madame, said the usher, it is the second movement of Beethoven's Fifth Symphony.

After the theatre, I sought the hotel where I had sent my baggage. The clerk scowled.

"What do you want?" he asked.

Rest, I said.

[7] "On Being Crazy," *The Crisis*, XXVI (June 1923), 56–57.

"This is a white hotel," he said.

I looked around. Such a color scheme requires a great deal of cleaning, I said, but I don't know that I object.

"We object," said he.

Then why——, I began, but he interrupted.

"We don't keep 'niggers,' " he said, "we don't want social equality."

Neither do I. I replied gently, I want a bed.

I walked thoughtfully to the train. I'll take a sleeper through Texas. I'm a bit dissatisfied with this town.

"Can't sell you one."

I only want to hire it, said I, for a couple of nights.

"Can't sell you a sleeper in Texas," he maintained. "They consider that social equality."

I consider it barbarism, I said, and I think I'll walk.

Walking, I met a wayfarer who immediately walked to the other side of the road where it was muddy. I asked his reasons.

" 'Niggers' is dirty," he said.

So is mud, said I. Moreover I added, I am not as dirty as you—at least, not yet.

"But you're a 'nigger,' ain't you?" he asked.

My grandfather was so-called.

"Well then!" he answered triumphantly.

Do you live in the South? I persisted, pleasantly.

"Sure," he growled, "and starve there."

I should think you and the Negroes might get together and vote out starvation.

"We don't let them vote."

We? Why not? I said in surprise.

" 'Niggers' is too ignorant to vote."

But, I said, I am not so ignorant as you.

"But you're a 'nigger.' "

Yes, I'm certainly what you mean by that.

"Well then!" he returned, with that curiously inconsequential note of triumph. "Moreover," he said, "I don't want my sister to marry a nigger."

I had not seen his sister, so I merely murmured, let her say, no.

"By God you shan't marry her, even if she said yes."

But,—but I don't want to marry her, I answered a little perturbed at the personal turn.

"Why not!" he yelled, angrier than ever.

Because I'm already married and I rather like my wife.
"Is she a 'nigger'?" he asked suspiciously.
Well, I said again, her grandmother—was called that.
"Well then!" he shouted in that oddly illogical way.
I gave up. Go on, I said, either you are crazy or I am.
"We both are," he said as he trotted along in the mud.

3
Pan-Africa

        Writing in 1897, Du Bois not only embraced the concepts of negritude and Pan-Africanism, but also implored the black people of America, "the advance guard of the Negro people" of the world, "to realize that if they are to take their just place in the van of Pan-Negroism, then their destiny is not absorption by the white Americans." Three years later, at the Pan-African Congress in London, Du Bois was the author of the Congress' address "To the Nations of the World." Urging self-determination for the black peoples of the world, he proclaimed at that time that "the problem of the twentieth century is the problem of the color line. . . ." World War I rekindled Du Bois' enthusiasm for Pan-Africanism, and in 1921 he wrote the most definitive statement of the movement's aims: "Manifesto of the Second Pan-African Congress." Two years later, Du Bois visited Africa for the first time. Several observers have criticized Du Bois for being excessively "romantic" in his attachment to the land of some of his forebears; and it was obvious, as he wrote in 1924, that "the spell of Africa is upon me." At the same time, Du Bois was extremely critical of the leading proponent of the "back-to-Africa" movement in the 1920's, Marcus Garvey, who, Du Bois argued, was either "a lunatic or a traitor." Du Bois' popular appeal never matched or even approached that of Garvey in his heyday, for the members of Du Bois' Pan-African Congresses of 1919 and the 1920's were actually worldwide representatives of the elitist Talented Tenth; in a way, the Congresses were like international extensions of the Niagara Movement. Garvey's Universal Negro Improvement Association, on the other hand, was different both in composition and appeal. It was, as George Padmore, Du Bois' longtime friend and fellow Pan-Africanist, has noted, "a people's movement rather than a movement of intellectuals." Although in conflict intellectually, ideologically, and temperamentally, both Du Bois and Garvey were pioneering Pan-Africanists, and both have justifiably been honored as such. In 1958, for example, Kwame Nkrumah hailed Du Bois and Garvey as "Sons of Africa" in his address to the All-African

People's Conference meeting in Ghana. "These [black] sons and daughters [of Africa]," Nkrumah declared, "were taken away from our shores and despite all centuries which have separated us they have not forgotten their ancestral links. . . . Many of them have made no small contribution to the cause of African freedom. Names which spring immediately to mind in this connection are those of Marcus Garvey and Dr. W.E.B. Du Bois. . . ."

"THE PROBLEM OF THE TWENTIETH CENTURY IS. . . ."[1]

In the metropolis of the modern world, in this the closing year of the nineteenth century, there has been assembled a congress of men and women of African blood, to deliberate solemnly upon the present situation and outlook of the darker races of mankind. The problem of the twentieth century is the problem of the color-line, the question as to how far differences of race—which show themselves chiefly in the color of the skin and the texture of the hair—will hereafter be made the basis of denying to over half the world the right of sharing to their utmost ability the opportunities and privileges of modern civilization.

To be sure, the darker races are today the least advanced in culture according to European standards. This has not, however, always been the case in the past, and certainly the world's history, both ancient and modern, has given many instances of no despicable ability and capacity among the blackest races of men.

In any case, the modern world must remember that in this age when the ends of the world are being brought so near together the millions of black men in Africa, America, and the Islands of the Sea, not to speak of the brown and yellow myriads elsewhere, are bound to have a great influence upon the world in the future, by reason of sheer numbers and physical contact. If now the world of culture bends itself towards giving Negroes and other dark men the largest and broadest opportunity for education and self-development, then this contact and influence is bound to have a beneficial effect upon the world and hasten human progress. But, if, by reason of carelessness, prejudice, greed and injustice, the black world is to be exploited and ravished and degraded, the results must be deplorable, if not fatal—not simply to them, but to the

---

[1] *To the Nations of the World,* Address of the Pan-African Congress (London: leaflet, 1900).

high ideals of justice, freedom and culture which a thousand years of Christian civilization have held before Europe.

And now, therefore, to these ideals of civilization, to the broader humanity of the followers of the Prince of Peace, we, the men and women of Africa in world congress assembled, do now solemnly appeal:

Let the world take no backward step in that slow but sure progress which has successively refused to let the spirit of class, of caste, of privilege, or of birth, debar from life, liberty and the pursuit of happiness a striving human soul.

Let not color or race be a feature of distinction between white and black men, regardless of worth or ability.

Let not the natives of Africa be sacrificed to the greed of gold, their liberties taken away, their family life debauched, their just aspirations repressed, and avenues of advancement and culture taken from them.

Let not the cloak of Christian missionary enterprise be allowed in the future, as so often in the past, to hide the ruthless economic exploitation and political downfall of less developed nations, whose chief fault has been reliance on the plighted faith of the Christian church.

Let the British nation, the first modern champion of Negro freedom, . . . give, as soon as practicable, the rights of responsible government to the black colonies of Africa and the West Indies.

Let not the spirit of Garrison, Phillips, and Douglass wholly die out in America; may the conscience of a great nation rise and rebuke all dishonesty and unrighteous oppression toward the American Negro, and grant to him the right of franchise, security of person and property, and generous recognition of the great work he has accomplished in a generation toward raising nine millions of human beings from slavery to manhood.

Let the German Empire, and the French Republic, true to their great past, remember that the true worth of colonies lies in their prosperity and progress, and that justice, impartial alike to black and white, is the first element of prosperity.

Let the Congo Free State become a great central Negro State of the world, and let its prosperity be counted not simply in cash and commerce, but in the happiness and true advancement of its black people.

Let the nations of the World respect the integrity and independence of the free Negro States of Abyssinia, Liberia, Haiti, and the rest, and let the inhabitants of these States, the independent tribes of Africa, the Negroes of the West Indies and America, and the black subjects of all nations take courage, strike ceaselessly, and fight bravely, that they may prove to the world their incontestible right to be counted among the great brotherhood of mankind.

Thus we appeal with boldness and confidence to the Great Powers of the civilized world, trusting in the wide spirit of humanity, and the deep sense of justice of our age, for a generous recognition of the righteousness of our cause.

MANIFESTO OF THE SECOND PAN-AFRICAN CONGRESS [2]

The absolute equality of races,—physical, political and social —is the founding stone of world peace and human advancement. No one denies great differences of gift, capacity and attainment among individuals of all races, but the voice of science, religion and practical politics is one in denying the God-appointed existence of super-races, or of races naturally and inevitably and eternally inferior.

That in the vast range of time, one group should in its industrial technique, or social organization, or spiritual vision, lag a few hundred years behind another, or forge fitfully ahead, or come to differ decidedly in thought, deed and ideal, is proof of the essential richness and variety of human nature, rather than proof of the co-existence of demi-gods and apes in human form. The doctrine of racial equality does not interfere with individual liberty, rather, it fulfils it. And of all the various criteria by which masses of men have in the past been prejudged and classified, that of the color of the skin and texture of the hair, is surely the most adventitious and idiotic.

It is the duty of the world to assist in every way the advance of the backward and suppressed groups of mankind. The rise of all men is a menace to no one and is the highest human ideal; it is not an altruistic benevolence, but the one road to world salvation.

For the purpose of raising such peoples to intelligence, self-knowledge and self-control, their intelligentsia of right ought to be recognized as the natural leaders of their groups.

The insidious and dishonorable propaganda, which, for selfish ends, so distorts and denies facts as to represent the advancement

and development of certain races of men as impossible and unde-
sirable, should be met with widespread dissemination of the
truth. . . .

We who resent the attempt to treat civilized men as uncivilized,
and who bring in our hearts grievance upon grievance against
those who lynch the untried, disfranchise the intelligent, deny
self-government to educated men, and insult the helpless, we complain; but not simply or primarily for ourselves—more especially
for the millions of our fellows, blood of our blood, and flesh of our
flesh, who have not even what we have—the power to complain
against monstrous wrong, the power to see and to know the source
of our oppression.

How far the future advance of mankind will depend upon the
social contact and physical intermixture of the various strains of
human blood is unknown, but the demand for the interpenetration
of countries and intermingling of blood has come, in modern days,
from the white race alone, and has been imposed upon brown and
black folks mainly by brute force and fraud. On top of this, the
resulting people of mixed race have had to endure innuendo, persecution, and insult, and the penetrated countries have been forced
into semi-slavery.

If it be proven that absolute world segregation by group, color
or historic affinity is best for the future, let the white race leave
the dark world and the darker races will gladly leave the white.
But the proposition is absurd. This is a world of men, of men
whose likenesses far outweigh their differences; who mutually need
each other in labor and thought and dream, but who can successfully have each other only on terms of equality, justice and mutual
respect. They are the real and only peacemakers who work sincerely
and peacefully to this end.

The beginning of wisdom in interracial contact is the establishment of political institutions among suppressed peoples. The habit
of democracy must be made to encircle the earth. Despite the attempt to prove that its practice is the secret and divine gift of
the few, no habit is more natural or more widely spread among
primitive people, or more easily capable of development among
masses. . . .

Surely in the 20th century of the Prince of Peace, . . . there can
be found in the civilized world enough of altruism, learning and
benevolence to develop native institutions for the native's good,

rather than continue to allow the majority of mankind to be brutalized and enslaved by ignorant and selfish agents of commercial institutions, whose one aim is profit and power for the few.

And this brings us to the crux of the matter: It is the shame of the world that today the relation between the main groups of mankind and their mutual estimate and respect is determined chiefly by the degree in which one can subject the other to its service, enslaving labor, making ignorance compulsory, uprooting ruthlessly religion and customs, and destroying government, so that the favored Few may luxuriate in the toil of the tortured Many. . . .

The day of such world organization is past and whatever excuse be made for it in other ages, the 20th century must come to judge men as men and not as material and labor. . . .

What do those wish who see these evils of the color line and racial discrimination and who believe in the divine right of suppressed and backward peoples to learn and aspire and be free?

The Negro race through its thinking intelligentsia is demanding:

I—The recognition of civilized men as civilized despite their race or color

II—Local self government for backward groups, deliberately rising as experience and knowledge grow to complete self government under the limitations of a self governed world

III—Education in self knowledge, in scientific truth and in industrial technique, undivorced from the art of beauty

IV—Freedom in their own religion and social customs, and with the right to be different and non-conformist

V—Co-operation with the rest of the world in government, industry and art on the basis of Justice, Freedom and Peace

VI—The ancient common ownership of the land and its natural fruits and defence against the unrestrained greed of invested capital

VII—The establishment under the League of Nations of an international institution for the study of Negro problems

VIII—The establishment of an international section in the Labor Bureau of the League of Nations, charged with the protection of native labor.

The world must face two eventualities: either the complete assimilation of Africa with two or three of the great world states, with political, civil and social power and privileges absolutely equal for its black and white citizens, or the rise of a great black African state founded in Peace and Good Will, based on popular education, natural art and industry and freedom of trade; autonomous and sovereign in its internal policy, but from its beginning a part of a great society of peoples in which it takes its place with others as co-rulers of the world.

In some such words and thoughts as these we seek to express our will and ideal, and the end of our untiring effort. To our aid we call all men of the Earth who love Justice and Mercy. Out of the depths we have cried unto the deaf and dumb masters of the world. Out of the depths we cry to our own sleeping souls.

The answer is written in the stars.

"THE SPELL OF AFRICA IS UPON ME" [3]

Africa

I have just come back from a journey in the world of nearly five months. I have travelled 15,000 miles. I set foot on three continents. I have visited five countries, four African islands and five African colonies. I have sailed under five flags. I have seen a black president inaugurated. I have walked in the African big bush and heard the night cry of leopards. I have traded in African markets, talked with African chiefs and been the guest of white governors. I have seen the Alhambra and the great mosque at Cordova . . . and I am full, very full with things that must be said. . . .

The Place, the People

Africa is vegetation. It is the riotous, unbridled bursting life of leaf and limb. It is sunshine—pitiless shine of blue rising from morning mists and sinking to hot night shadows. And then the stars—very near are the stars to Africa, near and bright and curiously arrayed. The tree is Africa. The strong, blinding strength of it—the wide deep shade, the burly lavish height of it. Animal life is there wild and abundant—perhaps in the inner jungle I should note it more but here the herb is triumphant, savagely sure—such beautiful shrubbery, such splendor of leaf and gorgeousness of flower I have never seen. . . .

[3] "Africa" and "Little Portraits of Africa," *The Crisis*, XXVII (April 1924), 247–51, 273–74.

Sunday, January 13, 1924

I have walked three hours in the African bush. In the high bush mighty trees arose draped, with here and there the flash of flower and call of bird. The monkey sentinel cried and his fellows dashed down the great tree avenues. The way was marked—yonder the leopard that called last night under the moon, a bush cow's hoof; a dainty tread of antelope. We leaped the trail of driver ants and poked at the great houses of the white ants. The path rose and wound and fell now soft in green glow, now golden, now shimmery through the water as we balanced on a bare log. There was whine of monkey, scramble of timid unseen life, glide of dark snake. Then came the native farms—coffee, cocoa, plantain, cassava. Nothing is more beautiful than an African village—its harmonious colorings—its cleanliness, its dainty houses with the kitchen palaver place of entertainment, its careful delicate decorations and then the people. I believe that the African form in color and curve is the beautifulest thing on earth; the face is not so lovely—though often comely with perfect teeth and shining eyes,—but the form of the slim limbs, the muscled torso, the deep full breasts!

The bush is silence. Silence of things to be, silence vocal with infinite minor music and flutter and tremble—but silence, deep silence of the great void of Africa.

And the palms; some rose and flared like green fine work; some flared before they rose; some soared and drooped; some were stars and some were sentinels; then came the ferns—the feathery delicate things of grottos and haunts with us, leapt and sang in the sun— they thrust their virgin tracery up and out and almost to trees. Bizarre shapes of grass and shrub and leaf greeted us as though some artist all Divine was playing and laughing and trying every trick of his bewitched pencil above the mighty buildings of the ants.

I am riding on the singing heads of black boys swinging in a hammock. The smooth black bodies swing and sing, the neck set square, the hips sway. O lovely voices and sweet young souls of Africa! . . .

Africa

The spell of Africa is upon me. The ancient witchery of her medicine is burning my drowsy, dreamy blood. This is not a country, it is a world—a universe of itself and for itself, a thing Different, Immense, Menacing, Alluring. It is a great black bosom where the Spirit longs to die. It is life so burning, so fire encircled that one bursts with terrible soul inflaming life. One longs to leap against the sun and then calls, like some great hand of fate, the slow, silent crushing power of almighty sleep—of Silence, of immovable Power beyond, within, around. Then comes the calm. The dreamless beat of midday stillness at dusk, at dawn, at noon, always. Things move—black shiny bodies, perfect bodies, bodies of sleek unearthly poise and beauty. Eyes languish, black eyes—slow eyes, lovely and tender eyes in great dark formless faces. Life is slow here. . . . Life slows down and as it slows it deepens; it rises and descends to immense and secret places. Unknown evil appears and unknown good. Africa is the Spiritual Frontier of human kind —oh the wild and beautiful adventures of its taming! But oh! the cost thereof—the endless, endless cost! Then will come a day—an old and ever, ever young day when there will spring in Africa a civilization without coal, without noise, where machinery will sing and never rush and roar, and where men will sleep and think and dance and lie prone before the rising sons, and women will be happy.

The objects of life will be revolutionized. Our duty will not consist in getting up at seven, working furiously for six, ten and twelve hours, eating in sullen ravenousness or extraordinary repletion. No—We shall dream the day away and in cool dawns, in little swift hours, do all our work.

ON MARCUS GARVEY [4]

In its endeavor to avoid any injustice toward Marcus Garvey and his followers, THE CRISIS has almost leaned backward. Notwithstanding his wanton squandering of hundreds of thousands of dollars we have refused to assume that he was a common thief. In spite of his monumental and persistent lying we have discussed only the larger and truer aspects of his propaganda. We have refrained from all comment on his trial and conviction for fraud. We have done this too in spite of his personal vituperation of the editor of THE CRISIS and persistent and unremitting repetition of falsehood after falsehood as to the editor's beliefs and acts and as to the program of the N. A. A. C. P.

In the face, however, of the unbelievable depths of debasement and humiliation to which this demagog has descended in order to keep himself out of jail, it is our duty to say openly and clearly:

[4] "A Lunatic or a Traitor," *The Crisis*, XXVIII (May 1924), 8–9.

Marcus Garvey is, without doubt, the most dangerous enemy of the Negro race in America and in the world. He is either a lunatic or a traitor. He is sending all over this country tons of letters and pamphlets appealing to Congressmen, business men, philanthropists and educators to join him on a platform whose half concealed planks may be interpreted as follows:

That no person of Negro descent can ever hope to become an American citizen.

That forcible separation of the races and the banishment of Negroes to Africa is the only solution of the Negro problem.

That race war is sure to follow any attempt to realize the program of the N. A. A. C. P.

We would have refused to believe that any man of Negro descent could have fathered such a propaganda if the evidence did not lie before us in black and white signed by this man. Here is a letter and part of a symposium sent to one of the most prominent business men of America and turned over to us; we select but a few phrases; the italics are ours:

Do you believe the Negro to be a *human being?*

Do you believe the Negro *entitled to all the rights of humanity?*

Do you believe that the Negro should be taught *not to aspire to the highest political positions in Governments of the white race,* but to such positions among his own race in a Government of his own?

Would you help morally *or otherwise* to bring about such a possibility? Do you believe that the Negro should be *encouraged to aspire* to the highest industrial and commercial positions in the countries of the white man in competition with him and to his exclusion?

Do you believe that the Negro should be encouraged to regard and *respect the rights of all other races* in the same manner as other races would respect the rights of the Negro[?]

The pamphlets include one of the worst articles recently written *by a Southern white man* advocating the deportation of American Negroes to Liberia and several articles by Garvery and his friends. From one of Garvey's articles we abstract one phrase:

"THE WHITE RACE CAN BEST HELP THE NEGRO BY TELLING HIM THE TRUTH, AND NOT BY FLATTERING HIM INTO BELIEVING THAT HE IS AS GOOD AS ANY WHITE MAN."

Not even Tom Dixon or Ben Tillman or the hatefulest enemies of the Negro have ever stooped to a more vicious campaign than

Marcus Garvey, sane or insane, is carrying on. He is not attacking white prejudice, he is grovelling before it and applauding it; his only attack is on men of his own race who are striving for freedom; his only contempt is for Negroes; his only threats are for black blood. And this leads us to a few plain words:

1. No Negro in America ever had a fairer and more patient trial than Marcus Garvey. He convicted himself by his own admissions, his swaggering monkey-shines in the court room with monocle and long tailed coat and his insults to the judge and prosecuting attorney.

2. Marcus Garvey was long refused bail, not because of his color, but because of the repeated threats and cold blooded assaults charged against his organization. He himself openly threatened to "get" the District Attorney. His followers had repeatedly to be warned from intimidating witnesses and one was sent to jail therefor. One of his former trusted officials after being put out of the Garvey organization brought the long concealed cash account of the organization to this office and we published it. Within two weeks the man was shot in the back in New Orleans and killed. We know nothing of Garvey's personal connection with these cases but we do know that today his former representative lies in jail in Liberia sentenced to death for murder. The District Attorney believed that Garvey's "army" had arms and ammunition and was prepared to "shoot up" colored Harlem if he was released. For these and no other reasons Garvey was held in the Tombs so long without bail and until he had made abject promises, apologizing to the judge and withdrawing his threats against the District Attorney. Since his release he has not dared to print a single word against white folk. All his vituperation has been heaped on his own race.

Everybody, including the writer, who has dared to make the slightest criticism of Garvey has been intimidated by threats and threatened with libel suits. Over fifty court cases have been brought by Garvey in ten years. After my first and favorable article on Garvey, I was not only threatened with death by men declaring themselves his followers, but received letters of such unbelievable filth that they were absolutely unprintable. When I landed in this country from my trip to Africa I learned with disgust that my friends stirred by Garvey's threats had actually felt compelled to have secret police protection for me on the dock!

Friends have even begged me not to publish this editorial lest I be assassinated. To such depths have we dropped in free black

America! I have been exposing white traitors for a quarter century. If the day has come when I cannot tell the truth about black traitors it is high time that I died.

The American Negroes have endured this wretch all too long with fine restraint and every effort at co-operation and understanding. But the end has come. Every man who apologizes for or defends Marcus Garvey from this day forth writes himself down as unworthy of the countenance of decent Americans. As for Garvey himself, this open ally of the Ku Klux Klan should be locked up or sent home.

4
Racial Pride, Racial Prejudice, and the Need for All-Black Action

As is evident in The Conservation of Races (*1897*), *Du Bois, while still a relatively young man, had wedded himself to theories and programs of all-black organization and action to deal with the day-to-day hardships of Afro-American life. He was a civil rights activist, but at times he despaired of ever seeing true democracy and racial equality in America. He was doubtful, too, that some of the values of white America were worthy of emulation by blacks. Moreover, he was proud of his race—its history, culture, and promise for the future.*

In writing of "The Economic Future of the Negro" in 1906, Du Bois suggested implementation by blacks of "the group economy," which, he explained, "consists of such a cooperative arrangement of industries and services within the Negro group that the group tends to become a closed economic circle largely independent of the surrounding white world." The theme of "the group economy" and "the closed economic circle" was one to which Du Bois returned time and time again; it was the theme, moreover, that led to his rupture with the NAACP in 1934. While protesting against "Jim Crow," Du Bois not only realized but even boasted that an inadvertent product of white segregation was the "welding [of] 10,000,000 American Negroes into one great self-conscious and self-acting mass. . . ." Du Bois' "Immediate Program for the American Negro" (1915), was, in part, a demand for intraracial cooperation and unity, and, ultimately, for "black power." In 1919 he warned that "if the Negro is to develop his own power and gifts . . . , then he must unite and work with Negroes and build a new and great Negro ethos." Progressively throughout the 1920's Du Bois reiterated this theme, and in a speech in 1930 he hinted at the ultimate logic of his argument. Addressing the graduating seniors of Howard University, Du Bois stated: "A generation ago those who doubted our survival said that no alien and separate [black] nation could hope to survive within another nation [white America]; that we must be absorbed or perish. Times have changed." Perhaps through economic, political, and social cooperation and unity, there could be "A Negro Nation Within the Nation."

In June 1934, the very month that Du Bois resigned his editorship of The Crisis, *he wrote an article for that magazine in which he quoted from* The Conservation of Races. *"Have we in America," Du Bois had written in 1897, "a distinct mission as a race—a distinct sphere of action and an opportunity for race development, or is self-obliteration the highest end to which Negro blood dare aspire?" Obviously, his answer to the former question was in the affirmative and to the latter, in the negative. Writing thirty-seven years later, he concluded: "On the whole, I am rather pleased to find myself still in so much sympathy with myself."*

"ON BEING ASHAMED OF ONESELF: AN ESSAY ON RACE PRIDE" [1]

. . . In the years between emancipation and 1900, the theory of escape was dominant. We were, by birth, law and training, American citizens. We were going to escape into the mass of Americans in the same way that the Irish and Scandinavians and even the Italians were beginning to disappear. The process was going to be slower on account of the badge of color; but then, after all, it was not so much the matter of physical assimilation as of spiritual and psychic amalgamation with the American people.

For this reason, we must oppose all segregation and all racial patriotism; we must salute the American flag and sing "Our Country 'Tis of Thee" with devotion and fervor, and we must fight for our rights with long and carefully planned campaign; uniting for this purpose with all sympathetic people, colored and white.

This is still the dominant philosophy of most American Negroes and it is back of the objection to even using a special designation like "Negro" or even "Afro-American" or any such term.

But there are certain practical difficulties connected with this program which are becoming more and more clear today. First of all comes the fact that we are still ashamed of ourselves and are thus estopped from valid objection when white folks are ashamed to call us human. . . . I remember a colored man, now ex-patriate,

[1] "On Being Ashamed of Oneself: An Essay on Race Pride," *The Crisis*, XL (September 1933), 199–200.

who made this discovery in my company, some twenty-five years ago. He was a handsome burning brown, tall, straight and well-educated, and he occupied a position which he had won, across and in spite of the color line. He did not believe in Negroes, for himself or his family, and he planned elaborately to escape the trammels of race. Yet, he had responded to a call for a meeting of colored folk which touched his interests, and he came. He found men of his own calibre and training; he found men charming and companionable. He was thoroughly delighted. I know that never before, or I doubt if ever since, he had been in such congenial company. He could not help mentioning his joy continually and reiterating it.

All colored folk had gone through the same experience, for more and more largely in the last twenty-five years, colored America has discovered itself; has discovered groups of people, association with whom is a poignant joy and despite their ideal of American assimilation, in more and more cases and with more and more determined object they seek each other.

That involves, however, a drawing of class lines inside the Negro race, and it means the emergence of a certain social aristocracy, who by reasons of looks and income, education and contact, form the sort of upper social group which the world has long known and helped to manufacture and preserve. The early basis of this Negro group was simply color and a bald imitation of the white environment. Later, it tended, more and more, to be based on wealth and still more recently on education and social position.

This leaves a mass of untrained and uncultured colored folk and even of trained but ill-mannered people and groups of impoverished workers of whom this upper class of colored Americans are ashamed. They are ashamed both directly and indirectly, just as any richer or better sustained group in a nation is ashamed of those less fortunate and withdraws its skirts from touching them. But more than that, because the upper colored group is desperately afraid of being represented before American whites by this lower group, or being mistaken for them, or being treated as though they were part of it, they are pushed to the extreme of effort to avoid contact with the poorest classes of Negroes. This exaggerates, at once, the secret shame of being identified with such people and the anomaly of insisting that the physical characteristics of these folk which the upper class shares, are not the stigmata of degradation.

When, therefore, in offense or defense, the leading group of Negroes must make common cause with the masses of their own race, the embarrassment or hesitation becomes apparent. They are embarrassed and indignant because an educated man should be treated as a Negro, and that no Negroes receive credit for social standing. They are ashamed and embarrassed because of the compulsion of being classed with a mass of people over whom they have no real control and whose action they can influence only with difficulty and compromise and with every risk of defeat.

Especially is all natural control over this group difficult—I mean control of law and police, of economic power, of guiding standards and ideals, of news propaganda. On this comes even greater difficulty because of the incompatibility of any action which looks toward racial integrity and race action with previous ideals. What are we really aiming at? The building of a new nation or the integration of a new group into an old nation? The latter has long been our ideal. Must it be changed? Should it be changed? If we seek new group loyalty, new pride of race, new racial integrity— how, where, and by what method shall these things be attained? A new plan must be built up. It cannot be the mere rhodomontade and fatuous propaganda on which Garveyism was based. It has got to be far-sighted planning. It will involve increased segregation and perhaps migration. It will be pounced upon and aided and encouraged by every "nigger-hater" in the land.

Moreover, in further comment on all this, it may be pointed out that this is not the day for the experiment of new nations or the emphasis of racial lines. This is, or at least we thought it was, the day of the Inter-nation, of Humanity, and the disappearance of "race" from our vocabulary. Are we American Negroes seeking to move against, or into the face of this fine philosophy? Here then is the real problem, the real new dilemma between rights of American citizens and racial pride, which faces American Negroes today and which is not always or often clearly faced.

The situation is this: America, in denying equality of rights, of employment and social recognition to American Negroes, has said in the past that the Negro was so far below the average nation in social position, that he could not be recognized until he had developed further. In the answer to this, the Negro has eliminated five-sixths of his illiteracy according to official figures, and greatly increased the number of colored persons who have received education of the higher sort. They still are poor with a large number of delinquents and dependents. Nevertheless, their average situation in this respect has been greatly improved and, on the other hand, the emergence and accomplishment of colored men of ability has been undoubted. Notwithstanding this, the Negro is still a group apart, with almost no social recognition, subject to insult and discrimination, with income and wage far below the average of the nation and the most deliberately exploited industrial class in America. Even trained Negroes have increasing difficulty in making a living sufficient to sustain a civilized standard of life. Particularly in the recent vast economic changes, color discrimination as it now goes on, is going to make it increasingly difficult for the Negro to remain an integral part of the industrial machine or to increase his participation in accordance with his ability.

The integration of industry is making it more and more possible for executives to exercise their judgment in choosing for key positions, persons who can guide the industrial machine, and the exclusion of persons from such positions merely on the basis of race and color or even Negro descent is a widely recognized and easily defended prerogative. All that is necessary for any Christian American gentleman of high position and wide power to say in denying place and promotion to an eligible candidate is: "He is of Negro descent." The answer and excuse is final and all but universally accepted. For this reason, the Negro's opportunity in State directed industry and his opportunity in the great private organization of industry if not actually growing less, is certainly much smaller than his growth in education and ability. Either the industry of the nation in the future is to be conducted by private trusts or by government control. There seems in both to be little or no chance of advancement for the Negro worker, the educated artisan and the educated leader.

On the other hand, organized labor is giving Negroes less recognition today than ever. It has practically excluded them from all the higher lines of skilled work, on railroads, in machine-shops, in manufacture and in the basic industries. In agriculture, where the Negro has theoretically the largest opportunity, he is excluded from successful participation, not only by conditions common to all farmers, but by special conditions due to lynching, lawlessness, disfranchisement and social degradation.

Facing these indisputable facts, there is on the part of the leaders of public opinion in America, no effective response to our agitation or organized propaganda. Our advance in the last quarter century has been in segregated . . . institutions and efforts and not in effective entrance into American national life. In Negro churches, Negro schools, Negro colleges, Negro business and Negro art and literature our advance has been determined and inspiring; but in industry, general professional careers and national life, we have fought battle after battle and lost more often than we have won. There seems no hope that America in our day will yield in its color or race hatred any substantial ground and we have no physical nor economic power, nor any alliance with other social or economic classes that will force compliance with decent civilized ideals in Church, State, industry or art.

The next step, then, is certainly one on the part of the Negro and it involves group action. It involves the organization of intelligent and earnest people of Negro descent for their preservation and advancement in America, in the West Indies and in Africa; and no sentimental distaste for racial or national unity can be allowed to hold them back from a step which sheer necessity demands.

A new organized group action along economic lines, guided by intelligence and with the express object of making it possible for Negroes to earn a better living and, therefore, more effectively to support agencies for social uplift, is without the slightest doubt the next step. It will involve no opposition from white America because they do not believe we can accomplish it. They expect always to be able to crush, insult, ignore and exploit 12,000,000 individual Negroes without intelligent organized opposition. This organization is going to involve deliberate propaganda for race pride. That is, it is going to start out by convincing American Negroes that there is no reason for their being ashamed of themselves; that their record is one which should make them proud; that their history in Africa and the world is a history of effort, success and trial, comparable with that of any other people. . . .

There is no other way; let us not be deceived. American Negroes will be beaten into submission and degradation if they merely wait unorganized to find some place voluntarily given them in the new reconstruction of the economic world. They must themselves force their race into the new economic set-up and bring with them the millions of West Indians and Africans by peaceful organization for normative action or else drift into greater poverty, greater crime, greater helplessness until there is no resort but the last red alternative of revolt, revenge and war.

"SEGREGATION IN THE NORTH" [2]

If . . . the N.A.A.C.P. has conducted a quarter-century campaign against segregation, the net result has been a little less than nothing. We have by legal action steadied the foundation so that in the future, segregation must be by wish and will and not law, but beyond that we have not made the slightest impress on the determination of the overwhelming mass of white Americans not to treat Negroes as men.

These are unpleasant facts. We do not like to voice them. The theory is that by maintaining certain fictions of law and administration, by whistling and keeping our courage up, we can stand on the "principle" of no segregation and wait until public opinion meets our position. But can we do this? When we were living in times of prosperity; when we were making post-war incomes; when our labor was in demand, we perhaps could afford to wait. But today, faced by starvation and economic upheaval, and by the question of being able to survive at all in this land in the reconstruction that is upon us, it is ridiculous not to see, and criminal not to tell, the colored people that they can not base their salvation upon the empty reiteration of a slogan.

What then can we do? The only thing that we not only can, but must do, is voluntarily and insistently to organize our economic and social power, no matter how much segregation it involves. Learn to associate with ourselves and to train ourselves for effective association. Organize our strength as consumers; learn to co-operate and use machines and power as producers; train ourselves in methods of democratic control within our own group. Run and support our own institutions.

"THE ANTI-SEGREGATION CAMPAIGN" [3]

. . . Affirm, as you have a right to affirm, that the Negro race is one of the great human races, inferior to none in its accomplishment and in its ability. Different, it is true, and for most of the difference, let us reverently thank God. And this race, with its vantage grounds in modern days, can go forward of its own will, of its own power, and its own initiative. It is led by twelve million

[2] "Segregation in the North," *The Crisis*, XLI (April 1934), 115–16.
[3] "The Anti-Segregation Campaign," *The Crisis*, XLI (June 1934), 182.

American Negroes of average modern intelligence; three or four million educated African Negroes are their full equals, and several million Negroes in the West Indies and South America. This body of at least twenty-five million modern men are not called upon to commit suicide because somebody doesn't like their complexion or their hair. It is their opportunity and their day to stand up and make themselves heard and felt in the modern world.

Indeed, there is nothing else we can do. If you have passed your resolution, "No segregation, Never and Nowhere," what are you going to do about it? Let me tell you what you are going to do. You are going back to continue to make your living in a Jim-Crow school; you are going to dwell in a segregated section of the city; you are going to pastor a Jim-Crow Church; you are going to occupy political office because of Jim-Crow political organizations that stand back of you and force you into office. All these things and a thousand others you are going to do because you have got to.

If you are going to do this, why not say so? What are you afraid of? Do you believe in the Negro race or do you not? If you do not, naturally, you are justified in keeping still. But if you do believe in the extraordinary accomplishment of the Negro church and the Negro college, the Negro school and the Negro newspaper, then say so and say so plainly, not only for the sake of those who have given their lives to make these things worthwhile, but for those young people whom you are teaching, by that negative attitude, that there is nothing that they can do, nobody that they can emulate, and no field worthwhile working in. Think of what Negro art and literature has yet to accomplish if it can only be free and untrammeled by the necessity of pleasing white folks! Think of the splendid moral appeal that you can make to a million children tomorrow, if once you can get them to see the possibilities of the American Negro today and now, whether he is segregated or not, or in spite of all possible segregation.

5
Marxism, Socialism, and the Communist Party

Although Du Bois was a Marxist and at one time even a member of the Socialist Party, he had grave doubts about a key tenet of Marxian socialism—the possibility of genuine working-class solidarity in America's predominantly biracial society. Racial caste and economic class were in conflict, and, as Du Bois argued in a speech in 1910, the capitalists in America were keenly aware of the economic profits to be gained by exploiting race hatred. The

> *exploiting capitalist . . . says to his white laborers, "I am not in business for my health; I seek the cheapest competent labor. Larger and larger numbers of blacks are demanding work at low wages; if you are dissatisfied and continue to make trouble and demand too much, I will replace you by black men." He turns to his black laborers. "You are lazy and incompetent— unless you work harder and stop complaining, I will replace you with white men." This again leads each [race] to regard the other as the chief cause of low wages and unfair treatment. . . .*

And one of the results of such exploitation was racial violence, as was evident during the riots in East St. Louis, Illinois, in 1917, and Chicago in 1919. In Du Bois' eyes, both white capital and white labor—the exploiters and those who allowed themselves to be exploited—were the enemies of black people.

With the outbreak of the Russian Revolution in 1917, Du Bois began to think seriously about communism; but here, too, his opinions were mixed and ambivalent. Theoretically, the socialized aspects of life in the Soviet Union excited his interest and favor. Upon returning in 1926 from his first trip to Russia, he proclaimed that "if what I have seen with my eyes and heard with my ears in Russia is Bolshevism, I am a Bolshevik."

American communism, however, was a different matter. In

*the 1930's Du Bois had little but contempt for Communists
in the United States who, he contended, were cynical manip-
ulators of black people. "One of the worst things that Negroes
could do today," Du Bois wrote in 1936, "would be to join the
American Communist Party," for its members "believe, apparently, in immediate, violent and bloody revolution, and
they are willing to try any and all means of raising hell anywhere and under any circumstances. This is a silly program
even for white men. For American colored men, it is suicide."*

*For their part, the Communists returned Du Bois' contempt
in full measure. In response to Du Bois' article "The Negro
and Communism," published in 1931, the* Southern Worker
*charged that "the program of the Black Judases has finally
been put down in black and white by Du Bois. . . ." It was
obvious, the* Southern Worker *continued, that Du Bois and
other blacks in the NAACP had "become 'white man's niggers' "; for "as Du Bois and his cronies have shown in deeds,
their ambition is to further split the working class . . . for
which task they are gratefully supported by the white ruling
class." And two years later, when* The Crisis *published Du Bois'
"Marxism and the Negro Problem," James S. Allen of the
Communist Party replied: "Dr. Du Bois' statement essentially
exhausts the position taken by all petty-bourgeois Negro nationalists. . . ."*

*It was only during the Cold War era that Du Bois and
the Communist Party of the United States became reconciled
to and then embraced each other. (See Part I, Section Six:
"Cold War Criminal; Cold War Hero.")*

A SOCIALIST-OF-THE-PATH [1]

I am a Socialist-of-the-Path. I do not believe in the complete
socialization of the means of production—the entire abolition of
private property in capital—but the Path of Progress and common sense certainly leads to a far greater ownership of the public wealth for the public good than is now the case. I do not believe
that government can carry on private business as well as private
concerns, but I do believe that most of the human business called
private is no more private than God's blue sky, and that we are
approaching a time when railroads, coal mines and many factories
can and ought to be run by the public for the public. This is the

[1] "Socialist of the Path" and "Negro and Socialism," *The Horizon*, I (February 1907), 7–8.

way, as I see it, that the path leads and I follow it gladly and hopefully.

Negro and Socialism

In the socialistic trend thus indicated lies the one great hope of the Negro American. We have been thrown by strange historic reasons into the hands of the capitalists hitherto. We have been objects of dole and charity, and despised accordingly. We have been made tools of oppression against the workingman's cause—the puppets and playthings of the idle rich. Fools! We must awake! Not in a renaissance among ourselves of the evils of Get and Grab—not in private hoarding, squeezing and cheating, lies our salvation, but rather in that larger ideal of human brotherhood, equality of opportunity and work not for wealth but for Weal—here lies our shining goal. This goal the Socialists with all their extravagance and occasional foolishness have more stoutly followed than any other class and thus far we must follow them. Our natural friends are not the rich but the poor, not the great but the masses, not the employers but the employees. Our good is not wealth, power, oppression and snobbishness, but helpfulness, efficiency, service and self-respect. Watch the Socialists. We may not follow them and agree with them in all things. I certainly do not. But in trend and ideal they are the salt of this present earth.

"THE BLACK MAN AND THE UNIONS" [2]

I am among the few colored men who have tried conscientiously to bring about understanding and co-operation between American Negroes and the Labor Unions. I have sought to look upon the Sons of Freedom as simply a part of the great mass of the earth's Disinherited, and to realize that world movements which have lifted the lowly in the past and are opening the gates of opportunity to them today are of equal value for all men, white and black, then and now. . . .

I have always striven to recognize the real cogency of the Union argument. Collective bargaining has, undoubtedly, raised modern labor from something like chattel slavery to the threshold of industrial freedom, and in this advance of labor white and black have shared.

I have tried, therefore, to see a vision of vast union between the

[2] "The Black Man and the Unions," *The Crisis*, XV (March 1918), 216–17.

laboring forces, particularly in the South, and hoped for no distant day when the black laborer and the white laborer, instead of being used against each other as helpless pawns, should unite to bring real democracy in the South.

On the other hand, the whole scheme of settling the Negro problem, inaugurated by philanthropists and carried out during the last twenty years, has been based upon the idea of playing off black workers against white. That it is essentially a mischievous and dangerous program no sane thinker can deny, but it is peculiarly disheartening to realize that it is the Labor Unions themselves that have given this movement its greatest impulse and that today, at last, in East St. Louis have brought the most unwilling of us to acknowledge that in the present Union movement . . . there is absolutely no hope of justice for an American of Negro descent.

Personally, I have come to this decision reluctantly and in the past have written and spoken little of the closed door of opportunity, shut impudently in the faces of black men by organized white workingmen. I realize that by heredity and century-long lack of opportunity one cannot expect in the laborer that larger sense of justice and duty which we ought to demand of the privileged classes. I have, therefore, inveighed against color discrimination by employers and by the rich and well-to-do, knowing at the same time in silence that it is practically impossible for any colored man or woman to become a boiler maker or book binder, an electrical worker or glass maker, a worker in jewelry or leather, a machinist or metal polisher, a paper maker or piano builder, a plumber or a potter, a printer or a pressman, a telegrapher or a railway trackman, an electrotyper or stove mounter, a textile worker or tile layer, a trunk maker, upholsterer, carpenter, locomotive engineer, switchman, stone cutter, baker, blacksmith, boot and shoemaker, tailor, or any of a dozen other important well-paid employments, without encountering the open determination and unscrupulous opposition of the whole united labor movement of America. That further than this, if he should want to become a painter, mason, carpenter, plasterer, brickmaker or fireman he would be subject to humiliating discriminations by his fellow Union workers and be deprived of work at every possible opportunity, even in defiance of their own Union laws. If, braving this outrageous attitude of the Unions, he succeeds in some small establishment or at some exceptional time at gaining employment, he must be labeled as a "scab" throughout the length and breadth of the land and written down as one who, for his selfish advantage, seeks to overthrow the labor uplift of a century.

THE WHITE INDUSTRIALIST AND THE BLACK SCAB [3]

He sat in a massive arm-chair, before a carved mahogany desk. Beneath him lay a Turkish rug, and behind him, through the window, one saw his steel mills, minting millions.

"Yes," he said; "I recognize the new power of the Negro in Industry. He broke the steel strike for us!"

My heart stopped. Merciful God! It is to this, we have come. I saw the squalor and toil and endless hours of the stricken workman. I saw him sink beneath the murk, while at his throat were the hands of my people!

Then to my heart the blood came surging back. Why were these rivals wallowing in the swill and offal of the Steel Barons? Was the work so lovely and the pay so high? No; but because black peonage of the South is worse than the foreign white slavery of the North; because the black worker has small choice: to be lynched, to work for nothing in Georgia and Arkansas, or to be a scab in Pennsylvania. It's better to be a scab. But who forced on the black man this choice? Two men,—the White Worker and the Steel Baron. The white worker, when he said in the South, "You shan't vote," and when he said in the North, "You shan't join my Union! Or, if you do join, you're still a nigger, and I'm white."

In part, then, the guilt lies with the worker; but only in part, and, perhaps, when we think of ignorance and poverty,—in smaller part. The deeper, bloodier, guilt lies with those Masters of Industry, who today, yesterday, and tomorrow, plan to make the petty, human jealousies, hatreds, rivalries, and starvations of workingmen, the foundation of their colossal fortunes. They are the breeders of mobs and lynchings, of unrest and despair, of race war and class struggle. They stand above the squabble, like ringmasters cracking their whips, and at every writhing coil of the long snakelike lash, some white man mobs a "nigger," and some black man takes the bread from the white man's mouth. Thus, in vicious, unending circle, the hate and harm rise, mount, and spread.

[3] "Dives, Mob and Scab, Limited," *The Crisis*, XIX (March 1920), 235–36.

"JUDGING RUSSIA"[4]

There is no question but that a government can carry on business. Every government does. Whether governmental industry compares in efficiency with private industry depends entirely upon what we call efficiency. And here it is and not elsewhere that the Russian experiment is astonishing and new and of fateful importance to the future civilization. What we call efficiency in America is judged primarily by the resultant profit to the rich and only secondarily by the results to the workers. The face of industrial Europe and America is set toward private wealth; that is, toward the people who have large incomes. We recognize the economic value of small incomes mainly as a means of profit for great incomes. Russia seeks another psychology. Russia is trying to make the workingman the main object of industry. His well-being and his income are deliberately set as the chief ends of organized industry directed by the state. . . . Russia . . . is seeking to make a nation believe that work and work that is hard and in some respects disagreeable and work which is to a large extent physical is a necessity of human life at present and likely to be in any conceivable future world; that the people who do this work are the ones who should determine how the national income from their combined efforts should be distributed; in fine, that the Workingman is the State; that he makes civilization possible and should determine what civilization is to be.

For this purpose he must be a workingman of skill and intelligence and to this combined end Russian education is being organized. This is what the Russian Dictatorship of the Proletariat means. This dictatorship does not stop there. As the workingman is today neither skilled nor intelligent to any such extent as his responsibilities demand, there is within his ranks the Communist party, directing the proletariat toward their future dictatorship. This is nothing new. In this government "of the people" we have elaborate and many-sided arrangements for ruling the rulers. The test is, are we and Russia really preparing future rulers? In so far as I could see, in shop and school, in the press and on the radio, in books and lectures, in trades unions and National Congresses, Russia is. We are not.

Visioning now a real Dictatorship of the Proletariat, two ques-

[4] "Judging Russia," *The Crisis*, XXXIII (February 1927), 189–90.

tions follow. Is it possible today for a great nation to achieve such a workers' psychology? And secondly, if it does achieve it what will be its effect upon the world? The achievement of such a psychology depends partly upon Russia and partly upon Western Europe and the United States. In Russia one feels today, even on a casual visit, the beginning of a workingman's psychology. Workers are the people that fill the streets and live in the best houses, even though these houses are dilapidated; workers crowd (literally crowd) the museums and theaters, hold the high offices, do the public talking, travel in the trains.

Nowhere in modern lands can one see less of the spender and the consumer, the rich owners and buyers of luxuries, the institutions which cater to the idle rich. . . .

But it is the organized capital of America, England, France and Germany which is chiefly instrumental in preventing the realization of the Russian workingman's psychology. It has used every modern weapon to crush Russia. It sent against Russia every scoundrel who could lead a mob and gave him money, guns and ammunition; and when Russia nearly committed suicide in crushing this civil war, modern industry began the industrial boycott, the refusal of capital and credit which is being carried on today just as far as international jealousy and greed will allow. And can we wonder? If modern capital is owned by the rich and handled for their power and benefit, can the rich be expected to hand it over to their avowed and actual enemies? On the contrary, if modern industry is really for the benefit of the people and if there is an effort to make the people the chief beneficiaries of industry, why is it that this same people is powerless today to help this experiment or at least to give it a clear way? On the other hand, so long as the most powerful nations in the world are determined that Russia must fail, there can be but a minimum of free discussion and democratic difference of opinion in Russia.

There is world struggle then in and about Russia; but it is not simply an ethical problem as to whether or not the Russian Revolution was morally right; that is a question which only history will settle. It is not simply the economic question as to whether or not Russia can conduct industry on a national scale. She is doing it today and in so doing she differs only in quantity, not in quality from every other modern country. It is not a question merely of "dictatorship." We are all subject to this form of government. The real Russian question is: Can you make the worker and not the millionaire the center of modern power and culture? If you can, the Russian Revolution will sweep the world.

"THE NEGRO AND COMMUNISM" [5]

The American Communists have made a courageous fight against the color line among the workers. They have solicited and admitted Negro members. They have insisted in their strikes and agitation to let Negroes fight with them and that the object of their fighting is for black workers as well as white workers. But in this they have gone dead against the thought and desire of the overwhelming mass of white workers, and face today a dead blank wall. . . .

Thereupon instead of acknowledging defeat in their effort to make white labor abolish the color line, they turn and accuse Negroes of not sympathizing with the ideals of Labor!

Socialists have been franker. They learned that American labor would not carry the Negro and they very calmly unloaded him. They allude to him vaguely and as an afterthought in their books and platforms. The American Socialist party is out to emancipate the white worker and if this does not automatically free the colored man, he can continue in slavery. . . .

When, therefore, Negro leaders refuse to lay down arms and surrender their brains and action to "Nigger"-hating white workers, liberals and socialists understand exactly the reasons for this and spend what energy they can spare in pointing out to white workers the necessity of recognizing Negroes. But the Communists, younger and newer, largely of foreign extraction, and thus discounting the hell of American prejudice, easily are led to blame the Negroes and to try to explain the intolerable American situation on the basis of an imported Marxist pattern, which does not at all fit the situation. . . .

The persons who are killing blacks in Northern Alabama and demanding blood sacrifice are the white workers—sharecroppers, trade unionists and artisans. The capitalists are against mob-law and violence and would listen to reason and justice in the long run because industrial peace increases their profits. On the other hand, the white workers want to kill the competition of "Niggers." Thereupon, the Communists, seizing leadership of the poorest and most

[5] "The Negro and Communism," *The Crisis*, XL (September 1931), 313–15, 318, 320.

ignorant blacks head them toward inevitable slaughter and jail-slavery. . . .

American Negroes do not propose to be the shock troops of the Communist Revolution, driven out in front to death, cruelty and humiliation in order to win victories for white workers. They are picking no chestnuts from the fire, neither for capital nor white labor.

Negroes know perfectly well that whenever they try to lead revolution in America, the nation will unite as one fist to crush them and them alone. There is no conceivable idea that seems to the present overwhelming majority of Americans higher than keeping Negroes "in their place."

Negroes perceive clearly that the real interests of the white worker are identical with the interests of the black worker; but until the white worker recognizes this, the black worker is compelled in sheer self-defense to refuse to be made the sacrificial goat.

"MARXISM AND THE NEGRO PROBLEM" [6]

. . . Under these circumstances, what shall we say of the Marxian philosophy and of its relation to the American Negro? We can only say, as it seems to me, that the Marxian philosophy is a true diagnosis of the situation in Europe in the middle of the 19th Century despite some of its logical difficulties. But it must be modified in the United States of America and especially so far as the Negro group is concerned. The Negro is exploited to a degree that means poverty, crime, delinquency and indigence. And that exploitation comes not from a black capitalistic class but from the white capitalists and equally from the white proletariat. His only defense is such internal organization as will protect him from both parties, and such practical economic insight as will prevent inside the race group any large development of capitalistic exploitation.

Meantime, comes the Great Depression. It levels all in mighty catastrophe. The fantastic industrial structure of America is threatened with ruin. The trade unions of skilled labor are double-tongued and helpless. Unskilled and common white labor is too frightened at Negro competition to attempt united action. It only begs a dole. The reformist program of Socialism meets no response from the white proletariat because it offers no escape to wealth and no effective bar to black labor, and a mud-sill of black labor is es-

[6] "Marxism and the Negro Problem," *The Crisis*, XL (May 1933), 103–4, 118.

sential to white labor's standard of living. The shrill cry of a few communists is not even listened to, because and solely because it seeks to break down barriers between black and white. There is not at present the slightest indication that a Marxian revolution based on a united class-conscious proletariat is anywhere on the American far horizon. Rather race antagonism and labor group rivalry is still undisturbed by world catastrophe. In the hearts of black laborers alone, therefore, lie those ideals of democracy in politics and industry which may in time make the workers of the world effective dictators of civilization.

6
Cold War Criminal;
Cold War Hero

In 1944, when the NAACP invited him to return to the organization as an adviser on race relations and international affairs, Du Bois gladly accepted. Not only had Atlanta University retired him from its faculty, but the NAACP job was an opportunity to step again into the political arena, and this time to perform before a worldwide as well as a national audience. Even by the late 1930's, Du Bois had begun to shift the focus of his energies and intellect away from the tragedy of domestic racism and onto what he saw as the related but greater tragedies of worldwide capitalism, racism, and imperialism. He began to feel even more certain, for example, that the oppression suffered by blacks in the American South was just one more instance of the white imperialism that was so evident throughout the world, especially in Africa and Asia.

In statements in 1944 and 1945 Du Bois traced the links he saw among capitalism, racism, and imperialism. "In the past and the recent past," he explained in late 1944, "we know how the lure of profit from rich, unlettered and helpless countries has tempted great and civilized nations and plunged them into bloody rivalry." World Wars I and II were recent examples, but numerous others could be cited. In addition, "Negro slavery in America was the passing phase of a great world labor problem but on it was built a new imperialism." Imperialism, Du Bois continued, was "primarily economic," but it also had a vested interest in notions of the racial inferiority of non-white peoples. Imperialism "is a method of carrying on industry and commerce and of distributing wealth. As such it not only confines colonial peoples to a low standard of living [but also] encourages by reason of its high profit to investors a determined and interested belief in the inferiority of certain races. . . ."

But what about the United Nations? Could it not confront imperialism and battle for the human rights of all of the world's peoples? Du Bois' answer was pessimistic. According to the organizational proposals then being made for that body, he explained, not only would the United Nations be ruled by the major imperialistic powers, but also "there will be six hundred million colored and black folk inhabiting colonies owned by white nations, who will have no rights that white people are bound to respect." And was this not like the American South, where black people, having been disenfranchised, were without representation? Were not blacks in the South, like blacks in Angola or South Africa, a colonized people? Du Bois argued that they were, and in 1947, in An Appeal to the World, Du Bois petitioned the United Nations on behalf of the NAACP to exert pressure on the United States "to be just to its own [non-white] peoples." In the United States, as elsewhere in the world, Du Bois declared, capitalism and racism had conspired to deprive non-whites of their freedom.

As the Cold War threatened world peace in the late 1940's and early 1950's Du Bois contended that the United States was "fighting or preparing to fight in Europe, Asia and Africa —not against an enemy, but against an idea—against the rising demand of the working classes of the world for better wage[s], decent housing, regular employment, medical service[s] and schools for all." Conspicuously embodying this "idea," according to Du Bois, were two nations, the Soviet Union and Communist China. Aligned against these nations were "the powerful [people] who today own the earth. . . . They order us to fight an idea; to 'contain' and crush any dream of abolishing poverty, disease and ignorance; and to do so by organizing war, murder and destruction on any people who dare to try to plan plenty for all mankind." Du Bois was outspoken in his partisanship during the Cold War (as in his condemnation, before the House Foreign Affairs Committee in 1949, of proposals to rearm the nations of Western Europe); and his estrangement from the United States became ever more absolute.

In 1960, in "Whither Now and Why," Du Bois addressed himself to the two major components of his philosophy: black consciousness and revolutionary socialism. A year later, he had made application for membership in the Communist Party of the United States and had accepted President Nkrumah's invitation to reside in Ghana. And two years later he was dead.

AN APPEAL TO THE WORLD [1]

. . . [O]pposition to any democracy which included the Negro race on any terms was so strong in the former slaveholding South, and found so much sympathy in large parts of the rest of the nation, that despite notable improvement in the condition of the Negro by every standard of social measurement, the effort to deprive him of the right to vote succeeded. At first he was driven from the polls in the South by mobs and violence; and then he was openly cheated; finally by a "gentlemen's agreement" with the North, the Negro was disfranchised in the South by a series of laws, methods of administration, court decisions and general public policy, so that today three-fourths of the Negro population of the nation is deprived of the right to vote by open and declared policy.

Most persons seem to regard this as simply unfortunate for Negroes, as depriving a modern working class of the minimum rights for self-protection and opportunity for progress. This is true as has been shown in poor educational opportunities, discrimination in work, health and protection and in the courts. But the situation is far more serious than this: the disfranchisement of the American Negro makes the functioning of all democracy in the nation difficult; and as democracy fails to function in the leading democracy in the world, it fails in the world.

Let us face the facts: the representation of the people in the Congress of the United States is based on population; members of the House of Representatives are elected by groups of approximately 275,000 to 300,000 persons living in 435 Congressional Districts. Naturally difficulties of division within state boundaries, unequal growth of population, migration from year to year, and slow adjustment of these and other changes, make equal population of these districts only approximate; but unless by and large, and in the long run, essential equality is maintained, the whole basis of democratic representation is marred and as in the celebrated "rotten borough" cases in England in the nineteenth century, representation must be eventually equalized or democracy relapses into oligarchy or even fascism.

[1] *An Appeal to the World: A Statement on the Denial of Human Rights to Minorities in the Case of Citizens of the United States . . . and an appeal to the United Nations for redress . . .* (New York: N.A.A.C.P., 1947), pp. 1–14. Reprinted with permission of the National Association for the Advancement of Colored People.

This is exactly what threatens the United States today because of the unjust disfranchisement of the Negro and the use of his numerical presence to increase the political power of his enemies and of the enemies of democracy. The nation has not the courage to eliminate from citizenship all persons of Negro descent and thus try to restore slavery. It therefore makes its democracy unworkable by paradox and contradiction. . . .

In other words while this nation is trying to carry on the government of the United States by democratic methods, it is not succeeding because of the premium which we put on the disfranchisement of the voters of the South. Moreover, by the political power based on this disfranchised vote the rulers of this nation are chosen and policies of the country determined. The number of congressmen is determined by the population of a state. The larger the number of that population which is disfranchised means greater power for the few who cast the vote. . . .

Not only this but who is interested in this disfranchisement and who gains power by it? It must be remembered that the South has the largest percentage of ignorance, of poverty, of disease in the nation. At the same time, and partly on account of this, it is the place where the labor movement has made the least progress; there are fewer unions and the unions are less effectively organized than in the North. Besides this, the fiercest and most successful fight against democracy in industry is centering in the South, in just that region where medieval caste conditions based mainly on color, and partly on poverty and ignorance, are more prevalent and most successful. And just because labor is so completely deprived of political and industrial power, investors and monopolists are today being attracted there in greater number and with more intensive organization than anywhere else in the United States. . . .

If concentrated wealth wished to control congressmen or senators, it is far easier to influence voters in South Carolina, Mississippi or Georgia where it requires only from four thousand to sixteen thousand votes to elect a congressman, than to try this in Illinois, New York or Minnesota, where one hundred to one hundred and fifty thousand votes must be persuaded. This spells danger: danger to the American way of life, and danger not simply to the Negro, but to white folk all over the nation, and to the nations of the world.

The federal government has for these reasons continually cast its influence with imperial aggression throughout the world and withdrawn its sympathy from the colored peoples and from the small nations. It has become through private investment a part of the imperialistic bloc which is controlling the colonies of the world. . . .

Now and then a strong political leader has been able to force back the power of monopoly and waste, and make some start toward preservation of natural resources and their restoration to the mass of the people. But such effort has never been able to last long. Threatened collapse and disaster gave the late President Roosevelt a chance to develop a New Deal of socialist planning for more just distribution of income under scientific guidance. But reaction intervened, and it was a reaction based on a South aptly called our "Number One Economic Problem": a region of poor, ignorant and diseased people, black and white, with exaggerated political power in the hands of a few resting on disfranchisement of voters, control of wealth and income, not simply by the South but by the investing North.

This paradox and contradiction enters into our actions, thoughts and plans. After the First World War, we . . . . joined Great Britain in determined refusal to recognize equality of races and nations; our tendency was toward isolation until we saw a chance to make inflated profits from the want which came upon the world. This effort of America to make profit out of the disaster in Europe was one of the causes of the depression of the thirties. . . .

But today the paradox again looms after the Second World War. We have recrudescence of race hate and caste restrictions in the United States and of these dangerous tendencies not simply for the United States itself but for all nations. When will nations learn that their enemies are quite as often within their own country as without? It is not Russia that threatens the United States so much as Mississippi; . . . internal injustice done to one's brothers is far more dangerous than the aggression of strangers from abroad. . . .

ON AMERICAN MILITARISM AND WORLD WAR [2]

Dr. Du Bois. I appear here . . . to protest against the proposal for the United States to arm Europe for war. The Congress is asked to vote down payment of $1.5 billion together with unspecified sums in the future to implement the Atlantic pact.

This huge sum is not for education, although our schools are in

[2] U.S. House of Representatives, 81st Congress, 1st Session, Committee on Foreign Affairs, *Mutual Defense Assistance Act of 1949* (Washington: Government Printing Office, 1949), pp. 261–66.

desperate need of help. It is not for infantile paralysis which is sweeping the land, nor for cancer which is killing thousands. It is not for curbing and putting to work the mad waters of those great rivers which annually kill men, women, and children and destroy their homes, stock, and property, leaving muddy and stinking disease behind. This rich country has not enough money to spend for fighting ignorance, disease, and waste, or for the old-age security of its workers, but nevertheless is asked to spend a vast treasure to murder men, women, and children; to blind and cripple them and drive them insane; to destroy property by fire and flood; and for the third time in 50 years to jeopardize the whole edifice of civilization.

We are assured that these arms are for peace, not war—just as we were promised that the pact was for peace, not arms. None but the stupid believe this assurance. Mr. Acheson's logic is flawless for fools:

> Gentlemen, this is a pact for peace.
> Thank you, gentlemen; now arms for the pact, not for war but for peace, war for peace. Russia? We do not mention Russia. We just might fight Russia. It is simple, gentlemen.

We are asked to believe that this country is in danger of attack from Russia or that Russia is ready to conquer the world. We did not believe this when we asked 10,000,000 Russians to die in order to save the world from Hitler. We did not believe it when we begged Russian help to conquer Japan. We only began to believe it when we realized that the Russian concept of a state was not going to collapse but was spreading.

Assuming that you do not like and even fear Russian communism, by what right do we assume that it can be stopped by force? One idea seems to be that we can conquer the world and make it do our bidding because we are rich and have the atom bomb. Even if this were true it begs the question of the right and justice of our rule.

Why in God's name do we want to control the earth? Is it because of our success in ruling man? We want to rule Russia and we cannot rule Alabama. . . .

We sought to rule China and have just confessed our failure.

We set out to rule Germany and apparently our only result is surrender to the very forces which we fought a world war to subdue.

How have we equipped ourselves to teach the world? . . .

If we aim to rule the world we have got to learn to rule ourselves.

We have got to free our science from the control of the Army and Navy. We have got to make our schools centers of real learning and not of propaganda and hysteria. We have got to clear our minds of unreasoning prejudices. We who hate niggers and darkies, propose to control a world full of colored people. Will they have no voice in the matter?

Without exact and careful knowledge of this world, how can we guide it? Yet we know that our knowledge of the world today is fed to us by a press whose reporters say what the owners of the press order them to say. This is not the reporters' fault. If they want to eat they will write as they are told. It is our fault, who are unwilling to pay even 5 cents for our morning news. Big business which pays millions for control of news gets what it wants printed. We naively assume that what we read in our press is the whole truth, when a little reflection would convince us that we have in America no complete picture of what is transpiring behind the iron curtain. If we retort with the assertion that Russians are equally deceived as to conditions here, that is no excuse for us. Two wrongs never made a right and two lies do not spell the truth.

If all this ended in opinion, that would be one thing and time would answer it. But it threatens to end in war. We are asked to begin a Third World War on the assumption that we are the possessors of truth and right and able to pound our beliefs into the world's head by brute force. This is a crazy idea and it is worse than folly to try it. If we have to answer to human wealth and happiness we do not have to force men to believe it by atom bombs.

Ideas are seldom changed by force.

I will not say that war has never advanced mankind, but I will aver that in modern times it would be hard to prove that of 1,000 wars 100 had added to human progress.

What ever is true in the past, it is certain that today no world war can bring success to any nation.

Of course, we know this is true of war as usually fought, but we think that we can now fight by push-button and machine, that human beings will only be necessary in mopping up. We Americans will not fight, we will let John do it—John and Jacques and possibly Hans—while we pay the bill from such pockets as we can reach most easily.

This is crude self-deception and makes us today the most hated nation on earth. The world indulged in that dream when arrows were invented, when gunpowder was first used, when armored battleships and submarines appeared. It is a dream which never will be realized. No, the only cure for war is reason. We have got to know and study the facts and act so as to avoid force. Otherwise we are lost.

Let's face it. We fight China. We fight Russia. We win or lose or stalemate. If we win, what can we do with 150,000,000 Russians and 450,000,000 Chinese? What would we know in their case more than we knew in Germany or Japan? What would convert them to our way of life except their eventual belief in it? And is not belief, fact and reason, and not guns, our real recourse?

What hinders us from beginning to reason now before we fight? Why are we afraid to reason and wait and persuade? . . . We are afraid. For we stop logical thinking. We invent witch words. If in 1850 an American disliked slavery, the word of exorcism was "abolitionist." He was a "nigger lover." He believed in free love and murder of kind slave masters. He ought to be lynched and mobbed. Today the word is "Communist." Never mind its meaning in a man's mind. If anybody questions the power of wealth . . . [or] advocates civil rights for Negroes, he is a Communist, a revolutionist, a scoundrel, and is liable to lose his job or land in jail. And yet there is not today in this Nation an honest progressive citizen who does not share in his beliefs many of the basic ideas of communism.

I am a fellow traveler with Communists insofar as they believe the great ideals of socialism as laid down by the world's great thinkers since the seventeenth century: I believe in the abolition of poverty. I believe in curbing the social and political power of wealth. I believe in planned industry and more just distribution of wealth. There is in this body of belief nothing revolutionary, unless human progress is revolutionary. There is nothing which has not been advocated by the best thinkers in three centuries.

But what we are being taught to believe today is that Russian communism is not socialism but something dishonest, misleading, and eventually evil—while our capitalist system alone is light and truth.

Calling names does not settle this controversy. We call Russia an authoritarian state.

So are we. All states are and must be more or less slave states. They differ in degree of control over citizens and progressive states look forward to decrease of state control, and increase of individual freedom, but Russia, starting with 90 percent of illiteracy in 1917, could not start as a full, free democracy. Only educated people can rule successfully.

Russia showed her faith in democracy by promptly decreasing her illiteracy to less than 10 percent in 30 years.

We showed our belief in slavery by taking 86 years to reduce Negro illiteracy to 30 percent.

We rage at planned economy, but we have planned economy. It grows and sells our crops. It sets our wages and fixes our prices. It tells us what to manufacture and when, where to sell our goods, and where not.

But democracy has no part in it. Our planning is done by our plantation system, by the great trusts of steel, tin, and aluminum, by General Motors and the du Pont empire, by Standard Oil, by railroads with their fradulent bonded debt and watered stock, by Wall Street.

This planning is strictly in private hands until it breaks down. Then trust and railroad, bank, and big farm come crawling to the Government for relief.

That, we are told, is not socialism. It is patriotism.

Let us balance in a reasonable way the case of Russia and the United States. Russia has never attacked us. We not only have invaded Russia but have allowed our country to become the center of the most far-reaching verbal attacks on Russia. We are making the United States a refuge for every ousted landlord and exploiter, spy, and informer who hates Russia. We blame Russia for joining Germany in 1940. But we know that she did this only after the United States and Great Britain had refused her offers of alliance and she must join Germany or stand alone.

When Germany turned and treacherously attacked Russia, we awaited her annihilation with equanimity. When, to our surprise, Russia beat Hitler, we welcomed her help but took our own good time before easing her desperate struggle in the east by a western offensive.

We sought her alliance against Japan and courted her at Yalta because we did not dream Japan was so near collapse. And even then we yielded no more than Russia was able to take.

She kept faith with us in every promise at a greater cost than any other country paid. Yet we peremptorily ended her absolutely essential lend-lease and since 1945 have apparently sought every excuse to make war upon her.

Why do we want war with Russia and who leads this demand[?] We profess to want to protect western Europe against Russia. But it is western Europe which since 1917 has almost continuously attacked Russia. It was western Europe and the United States who after World War I seized countries long recognized as Russian and organized border nations like Poland for the expressed and declared purpose of using them eventually for conquering Russia. It was not imperialist expansion which led Russia to reannex the Baltic States and to secure by every means the close alliance of Poland and the Balkans.

The real reason for war on Russia is not her natural effort to protect her own borders but her effort to establish a Socialist state. Our country is ruled by incorporated wealth, incorporated so as to form a nonhuman person; protected by the fourteenth amendment, secure in organization and ownership of property and able to escape major taxation by hiring the best legal talent of the land. This wealth is forcing us into war. The people of the country do not want war. You do not want war. But somebody does want war, somebody with power and influence, who owns the press and controls radio, cinema, and theater. Somebody whose consequent ability to form public opinion has forced this country into hysteria and fear.

Who is this somebody? It is the group which control the corporate wealth of this land. They have made money out of war. They are making money out of the fear of war. They demand a third world war to ward off the depression which threatens their business and their wild waste of public taxation. The enemy of this power is the plan of Russia to found a state where this power of wealth will be curbed and destroyed. It is not a question as to whether or not Russia can do this, as to whether or not the present Russian state is or is not succeeding. It is the determination to compel citizens to believe this can never be done and that any attempt to curb the anarchy of rule by wealth is of itself a crime to be suppressed and not even discussed.

Gentlemen, make no mistake. Russia and communism are not your enemies. Your enemy, ruthless and implacable, is the soulless and utterly selfish corporate wealth, organized for profit and willing to kill your sons in order to retain its present absolute power. It is not our sympathy for the Balkans that is leading us to war. What did we care about the Balkans so long as western capital was making 75-percent profit out of oil and slaves? We kow towed to czars and splendid grand dukes so long as they held power. But when Russia drove out idle nobility and foreign exploitation and tried to build a state for the consumer and not the investor, then the world which lives on low wage and monopolized land and resources began to scream that this plan was impossible and criminal and must be stopped by force. But why? If communism cannot be made to work, it will fall of its own overweight. But it may succeed, and to stop any such chance you are asked to hurl the world into war.

The cost will be horrible. If we force Europe to a military race for arms her effort to recover will be nullified. Another war, even if victorious, will ruin Great Britain and France. And its eventual cost by increased taxation will throw the laboring classes of all the Americas into hopeless turmoil and despair. . . .

The hope of America, the hope of the world, is no more war. We have the cure for disagreement and mistake in the United Nations.

Once we forced the League of Nations on an unwilling world, then we refused because of petty internal politics to support our own child. It failed and war and depression resulted. We planned a United Nations, including our own provision for unanimity without which we would not join. Now, when we cannot have our own way in everything, we are ready again to sabotage our own handiwork and substitute war for persuasion.

If you vote this blank check, gentlemen, do not assume that you will decide when and where to fight. . . .

We can easily be in a third world war before you learn of it, if you vote these billions.

How does it happen that the United States today, reversing its traditional stand of centuries, is now siding with every reactionary movement in the world, with decadent Turkey, with royalist Greece, with land monopoly in Korea, with big business in Japan, with British Tories and Fascist Italy?

This is against our better impulses and saner judgment.

There is much in the Russian effort at social uplift, with which, if I knew it fully, I am sure I would not agree.

There is also much in our own way of life with which I strongly disagree.

No nation is perfect, with a perfect program, but every people have a right to try their way and no nation has more clearly earned her right to test the doctrines of communism than the Union of Soviet Socialist Republics.

Whether they accomplish their greater aims or whether a reformed capitalism, an American invention, will bring more human happiness, in either case, or in combination of both, socialism is the natural and inevitable aim of the modern world. It will grow out of the industrial revolution of the eighteenth century as flower from seed. Seeking to stop it by Red-baiting is stupid. Trying to stop it by war is crime.

Let the churches sit silent or yell for murder. Let the universities lead the witch hunt. Let the Government call every effort for social uplift subversive. You and I, gentlemen, know the truth. God give us guts to follow it.

"WHITHER NOW AND WHY"[3]

The American Negro has now reached a point in his progress where he needs to take serious account of where he is and whither he is going. This day has come much earlier than I thought it would. I wrote in 1940 a book called "Dusk of Dawn" in which I sought to record our situation in a period of change which I expected to last for another 50 years, but the second world war and the rise of socialism and communism has hastened the event and we are definitely approaching now a time when the American Negro will become in law equal in citizenship to other Americans. There is much hard work yet to be done before the Negro becomes a voter, before he has equal rights to education and before he can claim complete civil and social equality. Yet this situation is in sight and it brings not as many assume an end to the so-called Negro problems, but a beginning of even more difficult problems of race and culture. Because what we must now ask ourselves is when we become equal American citizens what will be our aims and ideals and what will we have to do with selecting these aims and ideal[s]. Are we to assume that we will simply adopt the ideals of Americans and become what they are or want to be and that we will have in this process no ideals of our own?

That would mean that we would cease to be Negroes as such and become white in action if not completely in color. We would take on the culture of white Americans doing as they do and thinking as they think.

Manifestly this would not be satisfactory. Physically it would mean that we would be integrated with Americans losing first of all,

[3] "Whither Now and Why," *The Quarterly Review of Higher Education among Negroes*, XXVIII (July 1960), 135–41. Reprinted by permission of the publisher.

the physical evidence of color and hair and racial type. We would lose our memory of Negro history and of those racial peculiarities which have long been associated with the Negro. We would cease to acknowledge any greater tie with Africa than with England or Germany. We would not try to develop Negro music and Art and Literature as distinctive and different, but allow them to be further degraded as is the case today. We would always, if possible, marry lighter-hued people so as to have children who are not identified with the Negro race, and thus solve our racial problem in America by committing racial suicide. More or less clearly this possibility has been in the minds of Negroes in the past, although not assented to by all. Some have stated it and welcomed it. Others have simply assumed that this development was inevitable and therefore nothing could be done about it. . . .

Today when the African people are arising to settle their own problems we are in [the] peculiar position of being in a group of persons of Negro descent who not only cannot help the Africans but in most cases do not want to. Any statement of our desire to develop American Negro culture, to keep up our ties with coloured people, to remember our past, is being regarded as "racism." . . . As I have said before and I repeat I am not fighting to settle the question of racial equality in America by the process of getting rid of the Negro race; getting rid of black folk, not producing black children, forgetting the slave trade and slavery, and the struggle for emancipation; of forgetting abolition and especially of ignoring the whole cultural history of Africans in the world.

No! What I have been fighting for and am still fighting for is the possibility of black folk and their cultural patterns existing in America without discrimination; and on terms of equality. If we take this attitude we have got to do so consciously and deliberately. This brings up a number of difficult problems which we will have to solve and make definite preparation for such solution.

Take for instance the current problem of the education of our children. By the law of the land today they should be admitted to the public schools. If and when they are admitted to these schools certain things will inevitably follow. Negro teachers will become rarer and in many cases will disappear. Negro children will be instructed in the public schools and taught under unpleasant if not discouraging circumstances. Even more largely than today they will fall out of school, cease to enter high school, and fewer and fewer will go to college. Theoretically Negro universities will disappear. Negro history will be taught less or not at all and as in so many cases in the past Negroes will remember their white or Indian ancestors and quite forget their Negro forebearers. . . .

To some folk this type of argument would lead to the conclusion that we ought to refuse to enter white schools or to clamor for unsegregated schools. In other words that we ought to give up the fight against color discrimination. I want, however, to emphasize that this not only is unnecessary, but impossible. We must accept equality or die. What we must also do is to lay down a line of thought and action which will accomplish two things: The utter disappearance of color discrimination in American life and the preservation of African history and culture as a valuable contribution to modern civilization. . . . What then can we do or should we try to do?

Negro parents . . . will have to at least temporarily, take on and carry the burden which they have hitherto left to the public schools. The child in the family, in specific organizations or in social life must learn what he will not learn in school until the public schools vastly improve. Negro history must be taught for many critical years by parents, in clubs by lecture courses, by a new Negro literature which Negroes must write and buy. This must be done systematically for the whole Negro race in the United States and elsewhere. This is going to take time and money and is going to call for racial organizations.

Negro communities, Negro private schools, Negro colleges will and must be organized and supported. This racial organization will be voluntary and not compulsory. It will not be discriminatory. It will be carried on according to definite object and ideal, and will be open to all who share this ideal. And of course that ideal must always be in accord with the greater ideals of mankind. But what American Negroes must remember is that voluntary organization for great ends is far different from compulsory segregation for evil purposes.

Especially and first there has got to be a deliberate effort made toward the building of Negro families. Our family organization has been left almost entirely to chance. How, when and where, the Negro boy and girl is going to meet and mate has been given no organized thought and in many cases the whole process has been deliberately ignored. Beyond that comes the primary question of

what a Negro child is to do in life. This has been taught only inci-
dentally and accidentally. The primary basis and end of life has not
been guided by proper tuition in social sciences, in economics or in
ethics, outside and beyond school; in the family and in religious
organizations.

The Negro race has got to impress upon its children certain fundamental facts. The normal human being must work and work
regularly to supply his wants, such legitimate wants as food, clothes
and shelter. In addition there must be creative activities such as we
understand under art and literature and then there must be systematic recreation for health, for normal satisfying of the sexual
instinct, for social contact, for sympathy, friendship, love and sacrifice.

In this matter of life vocation we Negroes have got to inculcate
in the minds of our children many objects to which white America
today is not only opposed but bitterly fights. . . . [For example, we
must teach them that] the true object of business should not be profit
but service. The service of collecting raw material, processing it for
consumption and bringing it to the consumer. For this service wages
should be paid, but vast unearned income should not be given to the
man who steals the land and takes from the laborer that which is his
due. This is increasingly the belief of civilized countries, but it is not
the belief of Western Europe nor of white America. The correct attitude toward vocations must then be taught increasingly in our
schools. Yet today in American schools and colleges, white and black,
Economics, Social Science, Money and Finance are not properly
taught, and especially most schools and colleges are afraid to teach
the remedies which socialism and Communism proposed for better
distribution of work and income; or to tell how the larger part of the
civilized world is adopting these methods of accomplishing these
things. . . .

The great American world of which we have for centuries been
striving to become a part and which has arisen to be one of the most
powerful nations is today losing its influence and that American
Negroes do not realize. There was a time when as leaders of a new
democracy, as believers in a new tolerance in religion, and as a
people basing their life on equality of opportunity, in the ownership of land and property, the United States of America stood first
in the hopes of mankind. That day has passed. I took a trip recently
that lasted nearly a year. . . .

I and my wife went abroad to Great Britain and Holland, to France and Czechoslovakia, to Sweden and Germany, to the Soviet Union and to the Chinese Republic. It was the most astonishing trip I have ever had. It radically changed my whole point of view. I saw first that America and its actions since the first world war was thoroughly condemned by the civilized world; that no other country was so disliked and hated. . . .

Outside this matter of feeling was my discovery that the world was going socialist, that most of the people of the world, Europe, Asia and Africa were either socialists or communists. No matter what our attitude toward socialism and communism may be, no matter how we judge the teachings of Karl Marx we must face the truth. Not only black but white Americans must know. We do not know.

The news gathering agencies and the periodicals of opinion in the United States are deliberately deceiving the people of the United States with regard to the rest of the world. For a long time they have spread the belief that communism is a crime or a conspiracy and that anyone either taking part or even examining conditions in socialist lands is a self-conscious criminal or a fool.

For decades now they have made Americans believe that communism is a failure. . . .

What we Americans want is freedom to know the truth and the right to think and to act as seems wisest to us under the democratic process; and what we have to remember is that in the United States democracy has almost disappeared. There is no use deceiving ourselves in that respect. Half of the citizens of the United States do not even go to the polls. Most Negroes are disfranchised. It is the considered opinion of the social scientists in America that the election which made Dwight Eisenhower president cost over $100 million and perhaps $200 million. Why does America need such an election fund? A democratic election doesn't need it and the United States needed and used it only for bribing voters directly and indirectly or frightening men from acting or thinking. This is what the rulers of the United States demand and those rulers instead of being individuals are organized corporations who suppress freedom, by monopolizing wealth.

If all this is true, it must be taught to our youth. It must be taught by teachers and instructors and professors and in that case we must face the fact that these teachers may lose their jobs. . . . We must then vote for socialism. We began this in the New Deal and then were stopped. But in Europe and Asia and also in Africa Socialism and Communism are spreading. Socialism will grow in the United States if we restore the democracy of which we have boasted so long and done so little. Here is where Negroes may and must lead.

This is my sincere belief, arrived at after long study, travel, observation and thought. Many disagree with me and that is their right. They have every opportunity to express their belief and you cannot escape listening to them and should not if you could. But they have no right to demand that you refuse to listen to the worldwide voice of socialism or to threaten you with punishment if you do listen. This is the first right of democracy.

I appeal to the [teachers] . . . first to teach the truth as they see it even if they lose their jobs. To study socialism and communism and the philosophy of Karl Marx and his successors. To travel in the Soviet Union and China and then to dare take a stand as they honestly believe whether for or against communism. To refuse to listen to American propaganda without also listening to the propaganda of communism and to give up teaching and go to digging ditches before bowing to the new American slavery of thought. Above all to do everything possible to stop war and preparation for war which is the policy of the present rulers of this nation and their method of stopping socialism by force when they cannot stop it by work nor reason.

APPLICATION FOR MEMBERSHIP IN THE COMMUNIST PARTY [4]

To GUS HALL,
Communist Party of the U.S.A.
New York, New York.

On this first day of October, 1961, I am applying for admission to membership in the Communist Party of the United States. I have been long and slow in coming to this conclusion, but at last my mind is settled.

In college I heard the name of Karl Marx, but read none of his works, nor heard them explained. At the University of Berlin, I heard much of those thinkers who had definitively answered the theories of Marx, but again we did not study what Marx himself had

[4] "The Logic of a Noble Life," *Political Affairs*, XLII (October 1963), 31–32. Reprinted by permission of the publisher.

said. Nevertheless, I attended meetings of the Socialist Party and considered myself a Socialist.

On my return to America, I taught and studied for sixteen years. I explored the theory of Socialism and studied the organized social life of American Negroes; but still I neither read or heard much of Marxism. Then I came to New York as an official of the new NAACP and editor of the *Crisis* magazine. The NAACP was capitalist orientated and expected support from rich philanthropists.

But it had a strong Socialist element in its leadership in persons like Mary Ovington, William English Walling and Charles Edward Russell. Following their advice, I joined the Socialist Party in 1911. I knew then nothing of practical socialist politics and in the campaign of 1912, I found myself unwilling to vote the Socialist ticket, but advised Negroes to vote for Wilson. This was contrary to Socialist Party rules and consequently I resigned from the Socialist Party.

For the next twenty years I tried to develop a political way of life for myself and my people. I attacked the Democrats and Republicans for monopoly and disfranchisement of Negroes; I attacked the Socialists for trying to segregate Southern Negro members; I [p]raised the racial attitudes of the Communists, but opposed their tactics in the case of the Scottsboro boys and their advocacy of a Negro state. At the same time I began to study Karl Marx and the Communists; I read *Das Capital* and other Communist literature; I hailed the Russian Revolution of 1917, but was puzzled at the contradictory news from Russia.

Finally in 1926, I began a new effort: I visited Communist lands. I went to the Soviet Union in 1926, 1936, 1949 and 1959; I saw the nation develop. I visited East Germany; Czechoslovakia and Poland. I spent ten weeks in China, traveling all over the land. Then, this summer, I rested a month in Rumania.

I was early convinced that Socialism was an excellent way of life, but I thought it might be reached by various methods. For Russia I was convinced she had chosen the only way open to her at the time. I saw Scandinavia choosing a different method, half-way between Socialism and Capitalism. In the United States I saw Consumers Cooperation as a path from Capitalism to Socialism, while England, France and Germany developed in the same direction in their own way. After the depression and the Second World War, I was disillusioned. The Progressive movement in the United States failed. The Cold War started. Capitalism called Communism a crime.

Today I have reached a firm conclusion:

Capitalism cannot reform itself; it is doomed to self-destruction. No universal selfishness can bring social good to all.

Communism—the effort to give all men what they need and to ask of each the best they can contribute—this is the only way of human life. It is a difficult and hard end to reach—it has and will make mistakes, but today it marches triumphantly on in education and science, in home and food, with increased freedom of thought and deliverance from dogma. In the end Communism will triumph. I want to help to bring that day.

The path of the American Communist Party is clear: It will provide the United States with a real Third Party and thus restore democracy to this land. It will call for:

1. Public ownership of natural resources and of all capital.
2. Public control of transportation and communications.
3. Abolition of poverty and limitation of personal income.
4. No exploitation of labor.
5. Social medicine, with hospitalization and care of the old.
6. Free education for all.
7. Training for jobs and jobs for all.
8. Discipline for growth and reform.
9. Freedom under law.
10. No dogmatic religion.

These aims are not crimes. They are practiced increasingly over the world. No nation can call itself free which does not allow its citizens to work for these ends.

W. E. B. DU BOIS

PART TWO

W. E. B. DU BOIS VIEWED BY HIS CONTEMPORARIES

7

The Du Bois-Washington Controversy

Du Bois' indictment of Booker T. Washington in The Souls of Black Folk *evoked a flurry of responses not only at that time but also during the years to follow. Two of the most provocative of the contemporary responses were by two controversial men: Kelly Miller, outspoken black educator at Howard University; and John Spencer Bassett, Southern white historian and editor of* The South Atlantic Quarterly. *Often reprinted, Miller's "Radicals and Conservatives" submits the historically questionable thesis that William Monroe Trotter, the fiery black editor of the Boston* Guardian, *had woven "a subtle net about W. E. B. Du Bois . . . and gradually weaned him from his erstwhile friendship for Mr. Washington, so as to exploit his prominence and splendid powers in behalf of the hostile forces." Despite its anti-Niagara Movement bias, Miller's article is perhaps the most perceptive contemporary discussion of racial ideologies in the early years of the twentieth century. Bassett's analysis of* The Souls of Black Folk *and of the ideological divisions between Du Bois and Washington is more conventional, but it is also very insightful and has been described by Elliott Rudwick as "the fairest analysis and evaluation of Du Bois' aims. . . ."*

It is interesting to note that, while Washington himself did not respond directly to Du Bois, the Tuskegeean's surrogates and other public spokesmen did make Du Bois a target of criticism. Many of these attacks were personal, not substantive. For example, when Du Bois resigned from Atlanta University to assume the editorship of The Crisis, *the Atlanta* Independ-

ent *commented upon "The Passing of Prof. Du Bois." His
"passing from among us," the newspaper stated, "is a blessing;
for as a factor in the development of character among Negro
youths in the South, his influence is more destructive than
constructive. . . ."* Because of Du Bois' alleged elitism and
exclusiveness, the "longer he remained in this community the
less service he rendered the community life and [he] became
a greater stranger among the people whom it was his duty
to serve." Nor was this all; not only was he disdainful of his
fellow blacks, he even made life more vexatious for them, for
"he believed in denouncing the people of the other race with
whom it was our duty to make peace and live in harmony."

Criticism of this nature dogged Du Bois throughout his
life, and its authors were not always Washingtonians. In 1929
a young black sociologist, Allison Davis, wrote that Du Bois
"knows less men and women of his race than any prominent
person in America, by reason of his aloofness and exclusiveness.
He elects to know no one and to serve his people at forty
feet range."

"RADICALS AND CONSERVATIVES" [1]

When a distinguished Russian was informed that some American Negroes are radical and some conservative, he could not restrain
his laughter. The idea of conservative Negroes was more than the
Cossack's risibilities could endure. "What on earth," he exclaimed
with astonishment, "have they to conserve?"

According to a strict use of terms, a "conservative" is one who is
satisfied with existing conditions and advocates their continuance;
while a "radical" clamors for amelioration of conditions through
change. No thoughtful Negro is satisfied with the present status of
his race, whether viewed in its political, its civil or general aspect.
He labors under an unfriendly public opinion, one which is being
rapidly crystallized into a rigid caste system and enacted into unrighteous law. How can he be expected to contemplate such oppres-
sive conditions with satisfaction and composure? Circumstances
render it imperative that his attitude should be dissentient rather
than conformatory. Every consideration of enlightened self-respect
impels him to unremitting protest, albeit the manner of protestation
may be mild or pronounced, according to the dictates of prudence.

[1] Kelly Miller, "Radicals and Conservatives," in Miller's *Race Adjustment:
Essays on the Negro in America* (New York: The Neale Publishing Co., 1908),
pp. 11–18.

Radical and conservative Negroes agree as to the end in view, but differ as to the most effective means of attaining it. The difference is not essentially one of principle or purpose, but point of view. All anti-slavery advocates desired the downfall of the iniquitous institution, but some were more violent than others in the expression of this desire. Disagreement as to method led to personal estrangement, impugnment of motive, and unseemly factional wrangle. And so, colored men who are zealous alike for the betterment of their race, lose half their strength in internal strife, because of variant methods of attack upon the citadel of prejudice. . . . Mr. Booker T. Washington is the storm centre about which the controversy rages. Contending forces have aligned themselves, in hostile array, as to the wisdom or folly of the doctrine of which he is the chief exponent. . . .

[Two of the leaders of the opposition to Washington are William Monroe Trotter, editor of the Boston *Guardian,* and W. E. B. Du Bois.] By his blunt, persistent assault on Booker T. Washington [Trotter] has focalized the more radical elements of the Negro race, and has made himself the most forceful personality that the Negroes in the free States have produced in a generation. He is irreconciled to his great foe. This intrepid editor saw clearly that the so-called radical Negroes were wholly wanting in organization and leadership. He chafed under the chide of having no concrete achievement or commanding personality as basis and background of his propaganda. His enemies sought to silence the loudsome pretensions of those of radical persuasion by the cry that they had founded no institutions and projected no practical projects. That the same might have been said of Garrison and Phillips was regarded as a barren rejoinder. It is difficult to found an effective organization on a protest. There is little constructive possibility in negation. Through the influence of *The Guardian,* Mr. Trotter has held together and inspirited the opposition to Mr. Washington. His every utterance leads to the Cato-like refrain: "Booker Washington must be destroyed." Conscious of his own lack of attractive personality and felicity of utterance requisite to ostensible popular leadership, Trotter began to cast about for a man of showy faculties who could stand before the people as leader of his cause. He wove a subtle net about W. E. B. Du Bois, the brilliant writer and scholar, and gradually weaned him from his erstwhile friendship for Mr. Washington, so as to exploit his prominence and splendid powers in behalf of the hostile forces.

The author of the "Souls of Black Folk" is also a Harvard man, and possesses extraordinary scientific and literary talent. Few men now writing the English language can equal him in linguistic felicity. He is a man of remarkable amplitude and contrariety of qualities, an exact interrogator and a lucid expositor of social reality, but withal a dreamer with a fantasy of mind that verges on "the fine frenzy."

Dr. Du Bois began his career, not as an agitator, nor as a carping critic of another's achievements, but as a painstaking investigator and a writer of remarkable lucidity and keenness. The men who are now extolling him as the peerless leader of the radicals were a few years ago denouncing him bitterly for his restrained and reasoned conclusions. It is almost impossible to conceive how the author of "The Philadelphia Negro" could have penned the "Second Niagara Movement Manifesto," without mental and moral metamorphosis. When Du Bois essays the rôle of the agitator, and attempts to focus the varied energies of his mind upon a concrete social emergency, it is apt to result, as did his "Atlanta Tragedy," in an extravaganza of feeling and a fiasco of thought. His mind being cast in a weird and fantastic mold, his place is the cloister of the reflective scholar. He lives behind the veil; and whenever he emerges to mingle with the grosser affairs of life we may expect to hear, ever and anon, that sad and bitter wail. Dr. Du Bois is passionately devoted to the welfare of his race, but he is allowing himself to be exploited in a function for which he is by nature unfit. His highest service will consist in interpreting to the white people the needs and feeling of his race in terms of exact knowledge and nice language, rather than as an agitator or promoter of concrete achievement. Trotter is the real guiding power of the "Niagara Movement," for he, almost by his single hand, created the growth that made it possible. Although we may hear the voice of Jacob, we feel the hand of Esau. Du Bois ostensibly manages the new movement, but when he dares to deviate from the inflexible intentions of Trotter, there will be war within, and victory will rest with the intrepid editor.

We need not feel surprised, therefore, that such picturesque points as Niagara Falls and Harper's Ferry figured in the "Niagara Movement," under the guiding mind of Du Bois. They were planned by a poetic mind. It is a poet's attempt to dramatize the ills of a race with picturesque stage setting and spectacular scenic effect.

At the call of Du Bois a number of men met at Niagara Falls, in August, 1905, and launched the "Niagara Movement" amid the torrential downpour of the mighty waters. In this gathering were some of the ablest and most earnest men of the Negro race. The call appealed mainly to those of vehement temperament, every one of whom was an avowed opponent of Booker T. Washington. An address was issued to the country setting forth in manly, pointed terms the rights of the colored race. The platform of the movement contained nothing new, and its dynamic was derived from dissent. It was merely a protest against American color discrimination, based upon Mr. Washington's alleged acquiescence. Many of the subscribers to the new movement had not, up to that time, been known for their activity in behalf of the race, and espoused the cause as "a cult" with all the wonted zeal and intolerance of new converts.

The second manifesto of this body, issued from Harper's Ferry, the scene of John Brown's martyrdom, is scarcely distinguishable from a wild and frantic shriek. The lachrymal wail befits the child, which has "no language but a cry." Verbal vehemence void of practical power to enforce demands in an ineffectual missive to be hurled against the stronghold of prejudice.

Another meeting has been called at Oberlin, Ohio, because of its stirring anti-slavery suggestiveness. We may expect a future session at Appomattox, so prone is the poetic temperament to avail itself of episodal and dramatic situations.

When the "Niagara Movement" grows out of the declamatory stage and becomes tempered by dealing with the actualities of the situation it will find its place among the many agencies working together for the general cause.

The radical and conservative tendencies of the Negro race cannot be better described than by comparing, or rather contrasting, the two superlative colored men in whom we find their highest embodiment—Frederick Douglass and Booker Washington, who were both picked out and exploited by white men as the mouthpiece and intermediaries of the black race. The two men are in part products of their times, but are also natural antipodes. Douglass lived in the day of moral giants; Washington lives in the era of merchant princes. The contemporaries of Douglass emphasized the rights of man; those of Washington, his productive capacity. The age of Douglass acknowledged the sanction of the Golden Rule; that of Washington worships the Rule of *Gold*. The equality of men was constantly dinned into Douglass's ears; Washington hears nothing but the inferiority of the Negro and the dominance of the Saxon. Douglass could hardly receive a hearing today; Washington would have been hooted off the stage a generation ago. Thus all truly useful men must be, in a measure, time-servers; for unless they serve their time, they can scarcely serve at all. But great as was the diversity of formative influences that shaped these two great lives, there is no less opposability in their innate bias of character. Douglass was like a lion, bold and fearless; Washington is lamblike, meek and submissive. Douglass escaped from personal bondage, which his soul abhorred; but for Lincoln's proclamation, Washington would probably have arisen to esteem and favor in the eyes of his master as a good and faithful servant. Douglass insisted upon rights; Washington insists upon duty. Douglass held up to public scorn the sins of the white man; Washington portrays the faults of his own race. Douglass spoke what he thought the world should hear; Washington speaks only what he feels it is disposed to listen to. Douglass's conduct was actuated by principle; Washington's by prudence. Douglass had no limited, copyrighted programme for his race, but appealed to the Decalogue, the Golden Rule, the Declaration of Independence, the Constitution of the United States; Washington, holding these great principles in the shadowy background, presents a practical expedient applicable to present needs. Douglass was a moralist, insisting upon the application of righteousness to public affairs; Washington is a practical opportunist, accepting the best terms which he thinks it possible to secure. . . .

"TWO NEGRO LEADERS" [2]

Two men, Booker T. Washington and William E. Burghardt DuBois, stand out as leaders of the negro race in America. Both of them are young men, teachers of negroes, and residents of the South. Both are possessed of fine minds and excellent training. Both have influence with their race and in a way are its most prominent leaders. Both are thoroughly honest in their purposes, and both are contributing greatly to the progress of American negroes.

But in some respects these two men are essentially unlike. President Washington is the son of a slave woman. He is a self-made man in the truest sense. His education was gotten from an industrial school. His work in life has been to spread abroad the desire for, and the opportunity of acquiring, industrial training. He has been mostly concerned with a life of action. He is not a notable student of books, although he has a wide knowledge of men. On the other hand Professor DuBois is a student. He represents in his early life in a New England village, and in his later career, the most intellectual side of the life of the American negro. He is a graduate of Fisk University and has a doctorate of philosophy from Harvard. He has written some books of a distinctively scholarly character and his position among the students of American social conditions is very good. To the general public he is not so well known as the president of Tuskegee; but to a small public of students he is known quite as favorably. He represents the negro in his higher cultural aspect just as the other represents him in his industrial career.

Between these two men there now appears to be a striking difference of view in regard to the future of the negro race. One of them has for a long time been widely known because of his peculiar policy. His views have found acceptance in all parts of our country and with all sections of our population. The general impression has been favorable to him. But now comes from the other a book [*The Souls of Black Folk*] which is written from an entirely opposite point of view. Its appearance in itself is interesting; but the fact that its author is a man of known ability and honest purpose makes it distinctly worth our while to ask what there is in this book, and how its message concerns the problem to solve which it is written?

What, then, does the president of Tuskegee stand for? He stands for a progress which shall begin with the things which are and from that point move onward. He realizes that the problem is a human one, to be wrought out by human agents and in the face of all the impediments of human opposition. The negroes themselves, upon whom he must work, are very weak human beings. To develop them is a process of strengthening which must conserve a hundred weak forces. They are a child race. To give them at once the liberty of adults would debauch them. On the other hand, the white people, in whose presence this problem must be solved, have certain pronounced views of their own in regard to it. Their views may or may not be the most enlightened or the most equitable views. They may be, in fact, all that Professor DuBois would call them, a mass of prejudices; but for all this they are real views, and President Washington feels that they must be dealt with in a sensible manner. They must not be antagonized blindly.

His manner of meeting the problem is this: The most powerful force in raising a race upward is economic progress. This is the basis on which all other progress is based. The negro needs this first of all. He is, moreover, a weak race in the presence of the stronger white race. He cannot win in a fight with the white man. It behooves him to keep on the friendliest terms with this stronger race. By so doing he will bring peace between the two, and peace will give the opportunity for advance on the part of the blacks. In politics, as he very clearly sees, negroes are as nothing. It is useless to say that he ought to have the constitutional rights which the national government has granted to him. He is not now able to hold these rights, and they will not be allowed him by his opponents. It behooves him, therefore, to let politics alone—and to stress the acquisition of wealth. Of all negroes who have undertaken to advise the race President Washington is the one who leans most to the white people. Yet he has received more criticism from the whites than any other prominent negro, and it is a fine tribute to his character that he still maintains his position in regard to the relation between the races.

Professor DuBois approaches the problem from the standpoint of ethical culture. He does not, in the first place, believe in the efficacy of the gospel of material wealth. The soul is more than the body. To give up the higher life, which many negroes have longed for, and to seek for riches only would be a backward step. It would be debasement of the soul. He would not object to the acquisition of wealth; but he would object to the notion that it should be put before the development of culture. A culture[d] life for the negro is no unnatural thing to him, who is, in fact, a very cultivated man. He raises a warning against the cry for industrial education. It is not the only thing or indeed the chief thing which the negro needs. His chief want is the greatest opportunity to develop in the truest way which is open to any other citizen of America.

A word which is continually in Professor DuBois's mouth is "The Veil." By this he means the fact that a negro is everywhere made to feel that he is unlike other people, and that there is something which shuts him out of the world of other people. It is race prejudice. Ever and anon the author comes back to this idea. . . . He makes us feel what an awful thing it is to be in America a negro and at the same time to be a man of culture. . . .

To the average negro the Veil is not so dark as to his highly cultivated brother. He does not pine for the society of white people. He finds company enough of his own standard among his own race. To him race prejudice means a dark reservoir of race antagonism cropping out in frowns, in Jim Crow cars, and in suffrage amendments. However much he may feel it, it is not so much as the man of culture feels it, who at every turn finds a locked door in his face. To meet this condition Washington proposes that the negro shall accept the "Veil," and glorify the negro race until it shall be no dishonor to be black. DuBois would chafe and fret, and tear his heart out. And as for us, who are a divinely appointed superior race, how much do we do to render the burden lighter to either the one or the other?

Some good people are already regretting that "The Souls of Black Folk" has been published. The book is, in their minds, a check to the good work done by institutions like Tuskegee and Hampton. It is, too, a sign that there is disagreement between two of the most prominent leaders of the negro race. "The Souls of Black Folk" is a most respectful criticism of the views opposite to it. It deals with President Washington personally in a thoroughly considerate manner. So far as being a sign of ill-will between the author and his opponent is concerned, there can be no apprehension from the contents of the book. As to the other point, which is the main point after all, the relative merits of industrial and cultural education, that is a debatable point, and on it we need as much light as we can get.

Unquestionably the vast majority of Southern negroes need industrial training and business competency more than anything else. Perhaps ninety per cent of them come within this class. Yet the negro needs his own leaders—for who will lead him if not those of his own race. If there is any force in the argument that the white race should have higher education in order to develop its own leaders, there is the same force in a like argument as applied to the negro race. In fact, the way of the negro is hard enough in the near future. In the raw democracy of the South, which has just lost the guiding influence of the old planter class, there is not that patriarchal feeling for the dependent race which existed twenty years ago. The new citizens and the new leaders are practical men. They have shown it by legally excluding the negro from the polls. What other step they may take does not appear. The negro ought to use every moment in putting himself in a self-supporting and self-directing condition. He will have in the future a severer competition than he has ever had in the past. He will need not only a mass of self-supporting individuals, but a large number of wisely taught leaders—men of great moral weight and men of broad character. If higher education will make such leaders—and who can deny it?—he ought not for a day to think of abandoning his higher education. It may safely be said that there will never go to the negro colleges and universities enough students to lessen materially the number of negro laborers. It is a fact, too, that most negroes do not comprehend the very terminology of higher education. But the exceptional negro does exist, and every day he is more frequently encountered; for him the door of opportunity ought to be kept open. If Professor DuBois has succeeded in calling attention to the importance of this side of the problem—a side which in the popularity of industrial education was likely to be forgotten—, his book has done good.

Another matter of apprehension in regard to "The Souls of Black Folk" is that it will counteract a better understanding between the races, which, it is said, has been progressing more or less in the South recently. But has there been any such progress in recent years? While the president of Tuskegee has been advocating peace, has not State after State adopted disfranchisement? Has not this same leader been made the object of the most bitter criticism? Is there as much good feeling between blacks and whites today as twenty years ago? On the other hand, the pacific policy is a good one; first because it is right for men to live in peace with their fellows, secondly because it is useless for the negro to attempt to take vengeance upon the white man, and thirdly because it teaches the negro forbearance and self-control. The cry of Booker Washington for peace is a good cry, even though it does not secure its object. It is good because of its effects on the negro, whom it will make more patient and more self-controlled. It is good, too, because in the long run it may find willing response in the ears of a few brave Southern people who do not love the crude animalism of the passion-wrought masses.

Professor DuBois's protest is not a violent one. It is the cry of a man who suffers, rather than the reproach of a man who hates. It is a plea for soul opportunity, and it bears the evidence that its author while he was writing realized the hopelessness of it all. It deals with a most important phaze of the negro question, a phaze which must be reckoned with in the final solution of it, if we ever have any final solution of it. . . .

Within the last six months there has been handed to me a book the title of which is "The Negro a Beast, or In the Image of God." . . . A more stupid book it is impossible to conceive; yet it is worth while to place it and its author side by side with "The Souls of Black Folk" and its author. Can a "beast" write a book like the latter?

8
The Era of World War I and the 1920's

During World War I and the 1920's, Du Bois was under fire from practically all sides—from white segregationists, black revolutionary Marxists, and black nationalists. On the floor of the U.S. House of Representatives, Congressman James F. Byrnes of South Carolina accused Du Bois of being a seditionary if not a traitor to his country. Left-wing black socialists A. Philip Randolph and Chandler Owen of The Messenger (self-proclaimed as "the only Radical Negro Magazine in America") denounced Du Bois for being reactionary and for failing to represent the "leadership of the brand of what he once pretended to be, but of what he now finds he is not—radicalism." And, finally, Marcus Garvey was unremitting in the 1920's in his dismissal of Du Bois as "purely and simply a white man's nigger." Even as late as 1935 Garvey continued to condemn Du Bois for his "treachery." Writing that it was "no wonder" that Du Bois had resigned from his position at the NAACP, Garvey asked: "Can he continue abusing the white man when the American Negro is at the white man's soup kitchen?" In the 1920's, Garvey continued, Du Bois had sabotaged self-segregation for blacks as espoused by the Universal Negro Improvement Association; now, belatedly, he had embraced this program for black independence. "The ignorance of Du Bois and the treachery of Du Bois sabotaged the one thing that would have saved the American Negro; but now, naturally, he is ashamed of himself and he has . . . withdrawn from the active line, because he has nothing to give. And who is there that can do better?" Garvey asked. Nobody. "All the leaders have been fools like Du Bois."

DU BOIS AS SEDITIONARY AND EVEN TRAITOR [1]

. . . It is evident that the leadership of [Tuskegee's Robert R.] Moton and others, who, following in the steps of Booker Washington, preached conservatism to the race, is now being challenged by a crowd of radicals who are appealing to the passions of the negroes and inciting them to deeds of violence. These radical leaders are urging their followers to resort to violence in order to secure privileges they believe themselves entitled to, and the recent riots indicate that many are accepting this bad advice. It is unfortunate that some negro leaders heretofore regarded as conservative have changed their attitude.

A fair illustration of this type is W. E. B. Du Bois, editor of the *Crisis Magazine*. Du Bois has heretofore rendered great service to his people by intelligent leadership. He has acquired influence over many thoughtful negroes, and therefore his capacity for evil is enlarged. The recent issues of his magazine are filled with appeals to the prejudice and the passions of the negro, which can have no other result than to incite him to deeds of violence. A fair example is an editorial in the May issue of the *Crisis* . . . where, under the headlines "Returning soldiers," he declares:

> We sing: This country of ours, despite all its better souls have done and dreamed, is yet a shameful land.
> It lynches. . . . It disfranchises its own citizens. . . . It encourages ignorance. . . . It steals from us. . . . It insults us.

To support each one of these statements he prints a short argument, concluding with the following:

> This is the country to which we soldiers of democracy return. This is the fatherland for which we fought! But it is our fatherland. It was right for us to fight. The faults of our country are our faults. Under similar circumstances we would fight again. But by the God of heaven we are cowards and jackasses if now that the war is over we do not marshall every ounce of our brain and brawn to fight a sterner, longer, more unbending battle against the forces of hell in our land.

[1] James F. Byrnes, in U.S. *Congressional Record*, Vol. 58, Part 5, 66th Congress, 1st Session (Washington: Government Printing Office, August 25, 1919), p. 4303.

We return.
We return from fighting.
We return fighting.
Make way for democracy! We saved it in France; and by the great
Jehovah, we will save it in America or know the reason why.

The espionage law still in force provides that one who shall will-
fully print, write, or publish any language intended to incite, pro-
voke, or encourage resistance to the United States, or who shall
publish any abusive language about the form of government of the
United States, shall be punished by a fine or imprisonment. If this
editorial, which refers to this as a "shameful land," charging the
Government with lynching, disfranchising its citizens, encouraging
ignorance, and stealing from its citizens, does not constitute a violation of the espionage law, it is difficult to conceive language suffi-
ciently abusive to constitute a violation. Believing this to be true,
I have called this editorial to the attention of the Attorney General, with the request that if in the judgment of his department it
does constitute a violation of the law, that proceedings be instituted
against Du Bois. No greater service can be rendered to the negro today than to have him know that this Government will not tolerate
on the part of a leader of his race action which constitutes a violation of the law and which tends to array the negro race against the
Government under which they live and under which the race has
made greater strides than it has under any other Government on
earth. [Applause.] . . .

DU BOIS AS REACTIONARY [2]

In conclusion let us say, that the Crisis has reached its crisis. It
no longer represents the opinion of the millions of Negroes of the
United States who are insisting upon justice without compromise
or apology. . . . The editor of the Crisis lacks (1) intelligence, (2)
courage, or (3) he is controlled. In our generosity, we would say
that he lacks all three, to a certain degree. . . . In very truth, he
lacks intelligence. We recognize, however, that Dr. Du Bois has more
intelligence than the Crisis manifests, but this is subordinated to
his rapidly waning courage. Third and last, he is undoubtedly con-

[2] "The Crisis of the Crisis"; "A Reply to Congressman James F. Byrnes of
South Carolina"; and "Du Bois Fails as a Theorist," in *The Messenger*, II (July,
October, and December, 1919), 12; 12–14; and 7–8. Reprinted by permission of
A. Philip Randolph.

trolled by the Capitalist Board of the National Association for the Advancement of Colored People. *If he lacks intelligence, he can't lead correctly. If he lacks courage, he dare not lead correctly. If he is controlled, he will not be permitted to lead Negroes, in their own interests.*

The problem of the Crisis is the problem of *intelligence, courage* and *control.* It is the *crisis of the Crisis.* The sooner its influence wanes among Negroes, the sooner will they have begun to pass their crisis. The chief problem of the American Negro today is the ridding himself of misleadership of all kinds, and especially that of so-called organs of public opinion.

. . . [Congressman James F.] Byrnes then goes on to make a little revelation even to The Messenger staff in stating: "It is unfortunate that some Negro leaders heretofore regarded as conservative have changed their attitude. A fair illustration of this type is W. E. B. Du Bois, editor of *The Crisis* Magazine." This strikes us as more than a revelation; it is a grave charge against Dr. W. E. B. Du Bois. While we know that Du Bois is conservative, reactionary on economic and political questions, and compromising in the face of cheap honors and extended epaulets, we had never thought of him as being satisfactory to a . . . [rabid segregationist] Congressman like Byrnes, until he wrote a little prose poetry on "Returning Soldiers," most of which was neutralized by contradicting statements in the same issue. We hope that Mr. Byrnes will never be able to find in our general position anything satisfactory while he holds his present point of view.

Of course, we agree with what Du Bois says about this being a shameful land. That it lynches, disfranchises, encourages ignorance, steals from us, insults us, are too evident to admit of contradiction. As to the balderdash which Du Bois holds out on its being our fatherland, of course, we understand that as one of Du Bois's neutralizing, saving clauses. That **we return** is a fact. That **we return from fighting** is a fact. That **we return fighting** has been demonstrated in Longview, Texas, Washington, D.C., Chicago, Ill., Knoxville, Tenn. We think, however, that a little tip might be given to you, Mr. Byrnes. That we return fighting is stating it too mildly. **We return fighting like hell against the hell in this land.** We return fighting for law against the anarchy which the Southern Bourbons of your ilk have unloosed upon our people. Chicago and Washing-

ton are indeed but little skirmishes and fights between irritated boys
compared with what may come in your own state any day unless the
rights and privileges, the lives and property of Negroes are protected by constituted authority. There is a sort of gentlemen's agreement among nine out of every ten Negroes in the United States
which in strength of determination, undaunted courage, unremitting
advocacy, unswerving purpose and inflexible resolution to stamp
out the vandalism of the South, compares most favorably with your
Irish brothers in their invincible aim and unfaltering intention to
throw off the yoke of British tyranny and oppression even though
the little island is drenched in blood and tears.

With respect to your recommendation that the Attorney General
indict Du Bois under the Espionage Law, we make a counter-
recommendation, that he strike at the root of the evil by enforcing
the 13th, 14th and 15th Amendments to the Constitution; that he
use the Federal law to stop the peonage in South Carolina and the
South generally; that he stop you and your ilk from stealing the
votes of Negroes; that he stop you from riding into Congress upon
Negro potential votes, not cast but counted, in criminal violation of
the Constitution of the United States. . . .

Under the caption—"Leading Negroes Analyze Color Tragedy,"
in the New York Sun, October 12th, William E. Burghardt Du Bois,
Editor of the Crisis, discusses several salient points of the Negro
problem. He begins by stating the problem, enumerating the different specific disabilities from which the Negro suffers. This, of course,
is done splendidly. But the character and scope of the problem is
not the unknown quantity in our social equation. This is known by
every man in the street, and any school boy is not incompetent to
state it. The only question that taxes the resources of sociologists,
is the discovery of principles and the invention of methods that are
calculated to effect a solution. It is here, where the Editor reveals his
utter and lamentable incapacity to think fundamentally. For instance, he makes the following observations upon the group of
Negroes known as "white folks niggers": "With the appearance of
this Radical group (referring to the New Negro Radicals), comes
the disappearance, practically, of another group of Negroes upon
whom the white South has placed great dependence. They were
known among colored people as 'white folks niggers' and their
business was to soothe the ruffled feelings of the colored people and

to flatter the arrogance of the white people. Negroes were told that duties came before rights, and that they were asking for more than they deserved. Whites were assured that the Negroes wanted nothing but the right to work at such wages as the white people wished to give them." No unusual power of penetration is necessary to perceive that this statement is both fallacious and vicious. It is fallacious in that it is not true, and it is vicious in that it is misleading. Everybody knows that that hand-picked, me-too-boss, hat-in-hand, sycophant, lick-spittling group of Negroes, appropriately dubbed "white folks niggers," have not disappeared, for they are now the recognized leaders of the Negro. For, according to the definition of "white folks niggers" as presented by Du Bois himself, in the above named article: "as those that soothe the ruffled feelings of colored people and flatter the arrogance of white people, play up duties and soft pedal rights and call for more work with any wages," fits the editor himself, since we have not known of any zealous efforts of his, in the interest of unionizing Negro workers to strike for more wages, shorter hours and better working conditions. . . . Du Bois proceeds in his past-time of misrepresentation of the attitude of the rank and file of Negroes by pretending that the National Association for the Advancement of Colored People is the expression of the aims and strivings of the Negro. In this connection he states that, "The mass of thinking American Negroes are represented by the National Association for the Advancement of Colored People and they stand with white Americans, who have given thought and attention to the Negro problem." This is absolutely false. The National Association for the Advancement of Colored People is led, controlled and dominated by a group who are neither Negroes nor working people, which renders it utterly impossible to articulate the aims of a group that are the victims of certain social, political and economic evils as a race, and as a part of the great working people. . . . The point of discussion in the above named article, however, which interests us most and reveals Du Bois' ignorance of theory and his inability to advise the Negro in the most critical period of the world's history, is shown by his view of "revolution." He says "that they (the Negroes) are deeply in earnest concerning this race problem, but it is hardly necessary to say that they do not believe in violence, they do not believe in revolution, they do not believe in retaliation, they do believe in self defense."

Doubtless Du Bois is the only alleged leader of an oppressed group of people in the world today who condemns revolution. In other words, he would continue to defend and maintain the **status quo,** or things as they are: the exploitation of labor by capital, which breeds wars and engenders race strife, fosters lynchings and riots and perpetuates a mockery of democracy. He would reject and renounce the right of revolution, which is even vouchsafed in so conservative a political instrument as the Declaration of Independence. Of course, we realize that his attitude to the idea of revolution arises out of his ignorance of its history and its relation to social progress. Capitalism, the present social order which he would maintain, only came after a revolution which effected the overthrow of feudalism. . . . The abolition of slavery, or the destruction of the rights of private property in human beings, was achieved through the mechanics of revolution. Our present industrial civilization, with its myriad labor saving devices and inventions for the utilization of the materials and forces of nature, was wrought in the laboratory of revolution. In short, every notable and worthwhile advance in human history has been achieved by revolution, either intellectual, political or economic. The overthrow of the Czar of Russia and the deposition of the Kaiser of Germany and the House of Hapsburg of Austria-Hungary are instances in proof of the genius of revolution, fashioning a new world for mankind. And yet, Du Bois, the supposed leader of the most ruthlessly and mercilessly exploited and oppressed peoples of the world, would reject the only hope of the Negro, as well as of mankind—"revolution." It is because he thinks it means violence, blood shed, a reign of terror, whereas, on the contrary, it means the abolition of the causes of these things—the system of private property in the social resources and machinery of wealth production. Du Bois continues, "that the Negro puts his greatest dependence in the essential decency and sense of justice of the American nation." If this were true, it would simply indicate the utter hopelessness of the Negro, for who would depend upon the American sense of justice to abolish lynchings, riots, disfranchisement and the jim-crow car, when this alleged sense of justice has condoned, sanctioned and connived at these outrages for almost a half century. This is the policy of the **Old Crowd Negro,** and it has failed, and failed miserably, to save the life and property of Negroes in America. . . . Du Bois is correct in one case, however, that is, when he says, "that we, who for twenty-five years have been called Radicals, were not in fact radicals at all." Indeed a belated admission but, nevertheless, he . . . is about to recognize that the times require leadership of the brand of what he once pretended to be, but of what he now finds he is not—radicalism.

DU BOIS AS "A HATER OF DARK PEOPLE"[3]

W. E. Burghardt DuBois, the Negro "misleader," who is editor of the "Crisis," the official organ of the National Association for the Advancement of "certain" Colored People, . . . has again appeared in print. This time he appears as author of an article . . . in which he makes the effort to criticize Marcus Garvey, the Universal Negro Improvement Association and the Black Star Line. This "unfortunate mulatto," who bewails every day the drop of Negro blood in his veins, being sorry that he is not Dutch or French, has taken upon himself the responsibility of criticizing and condemning other people while holding himself up as the social "unapproachable" and the great "I AM" of the Negro race. But we will see who Mr. DuBois is, in that he invites his own characterization. So we will, therefore, let him see himself as others see him.

"Fat, Black, Ugly Man"

In describing Marcus Garvey in the article before mentioned, he referred to him as a "little, fat, black man; ugly, but with intelligent eyes and a big head." Now, what does DuBois mean by ugly? This so-called professor . . . ought to know by now that the standard of beauty within a race is not arrived at by comparison with another race; as, for instance, if we were to desire to find out the standard of beauty among the Japanese people we would not judge them from the Anglo-Saxon viewpoint, but from the Japanese. How he arrives at his conclusion that Marcus Garvey is ugly, being a Negro, is impossible to determine, in that if there is any ugliness in the Negro race it would be reflected more through DuBois than Marcus Garvey, in that he himself tells us that he is a little Dutch, a little French, and a little Negro. Why, in fact, the man is a monstrosity. So, if there is any ugliness it is on the part of DuBois and not on the part of the "little fat, black man with the big head,"

[3] *Negro World*, February 13, 1923; reprinted in Amy Jacques-Garvey ed., *Philosophy and Opinions of Marcus Garvey* (New York: Atheneum ed., 1969), pp. 310–20. Reprinted by permission of Amy Jacques-Garvey.

because all this description is typical of the African. But this only goes to show how much hate DuBois has for the black blood in his veins. Anything that is black, to him, is ugly, is hideous, is monstrous. . . .

Du Bois and White Company

It is no wonder that DuBois seeks the company of white people, because he hates black as being ugly. That is why he likes to dance with white people, and dine with them, and sometimes sleep with them, because from his way of seeing things all that is black is ugly, and all that is white is beautiful. Yet this professor, who sees ugliness in being black, essays to be a leader of the Negro people and has been trying for over fourteen years to deceive them through his connection with the National Association for the Advancement of Colored People. Now what does he mean by advancing colored people if he hates black so much? In what direction must we expect his advancement? We can conclude in no other way than that it is in the direction of losing our black identity and becoming, as nearly as possible, the lowest whites by assimilation and miscegenation.

This probably is accountable for the bleaching processes and the hair straightening escapades of some of the people who are identified with the National Association for the Advancement of Colored People in their mad desire of approach to the white race, in which they see beauty as advocated by the professor. . . . It is no wonder some of these individuals use the lip stick, and it is no wonder that the erudite Doctor keeps a French Beard. Surely that is not typical of Africa, it is typical of that blood which he loves so well and which he bewails in not having more in his veins—French. . . .

Social Honors for Negroes

In referring to the matter, he says in the article: "Many American Negroes and some others were scandalized by something which they could but regard as a simple child's play. It seemed to them sinister. This enthronement of a demagogue, a blatant boaster, who with monkey-shines was deluding the people, and taking their hard-earned dollars; and in high Harlem there arose an insistent cry, 'Garvey must go!'" Indeed DuBois was scandalized by the creation of a Peerage and Knighthood by Negroes, and in truth the person who is responsible for the creation of such a thing should go, because DuBois and those who think like him can see and regard honor conferred only by their white masters. If DuBois was created a Knight Commander of the Bath by the British King, or awarded a similar honor by some white Potentate, he would have advertised it from cover to cover of the "Crisis," and he would have written a book and told us how he was recognized above his fellows by such a Potentate, but it was not done that way. This was an enthronement of Negroes, in which DuBois could see nothing worth while. He was behind the "Garvey must go!" program started in Harlem immediately after the enthronement, because he realized that Garvey and the Universal Negro Improvement Association were usurping the right he had arrogated to himself as being the highest social dignitary, not only in Harlem but throughout the country.

Marcus Garvey and His Birth and Du Bois

In the seventh paragraph of his article DuBois has the following to say: "Let us note the facts. Marcus Garvey was born on the northern coast of Jamaica in 1887. He was a poor black boy, his father dying in the almshouse. . . . He was poor, he was black, he had no chance for a university education, he had no likely chance for preferment in any line, but could work as an artisan at small wage for the rest of his life."

Now let us consider Marcus Garvey in comparison with DuBois. W. E. B. DuBois was born in Great Barrington, Mass., in 1868. Some wealthy white people became interested in him and assisted in his education. They sent him to Fisk University, from Fisk to Harvard, where he graduated as a commencement orator. . . . Where he was born—that is, in Great Barrington, Mass.—he had early association with white surroundings. He was brought up with white boys and girls of the better type and more aristocratic class as found in rural towns. He had no love for the poor, even the poor whites in his neighborhood, although he was but a poor, penniless and humble Negro. As proof of that he wrote the following on the tenth page of his book known as "Dark Water": "I greatly despised the poor Irish and South Germans who slaved in the mills (that is, the mills of the town in which he was born), and I annexed myself with the rich and well-to-do as my natural companions." . . . Admitting that Marcus Garvey was born poor, he never encouraged a hatred for the people of his kind or class, but to the contrary devoted his life to the improvement and higher development of that class within the race which has been struggling under the disadvantage that DuBois himself portrays in his article.

Comparison Between Two Men

Marcus Garvey was born in 1887; DuBois was born in 1868; That shows that DuBois is old enough to be Marcus Garvey's father. But what has happened? Within the fifty-five years of DuBois' life we find him still living on the patronage of good white people, and with the thirty-six years of Marcus Garvey's . . . he is able to at least pass over the charity of white people and develop an independent program originally financed by himself to the extent of thousands of dollars, now taken up by the Negro peoples themselves. Now which of the two is poorer in character and in manhood? The older man, who had all these opportunities and still elects to be a parasite, living off the good will of another race, or the younger man, who had sufficient self-respect to make an effort to do for himself, even though in his effort he constructs a "dirty brick building" from which he can send out his propaganda on race self-reliance and self-respect.

Motive of Du Bois

To go back to the motive of DuBois in the advocacy of the National Association for the Advancement of Colored People is to expose him for what he is. The National Association for the Advancement of Colored People executives have not been honest enough to explain to the people of the Negro race their real solution for the Negro problem, because they are afraid that they would be turned down in their intention. They would make it appear that they are interested in the advancement of the Negro people of America, when, in truth, they are but interested in the subjugation of certain types of the Negro race and the assimilation of as many of the race as possible into the white race. . . .

Now this is the kind of a settlement that he and the National Association for the Advancement of Colored People want in America, and they have not been honest enough to come out and tell us so, that we might act accordingly. This is why DuBois bewails the black blood in his veins. This is why he regards Marcus Garvey and the Universal Negro Improvement Association as impossible. This is why he calls Marcus Garvey "black and ugly." But . . . he must realize that the fifteen million Negroes in the United States of America do not desire such a settlement; that outside of himself and a half-dozen men of his school of thought, who make up the Executive of the National Association for the Advancement of Colored People, the majority of Negroes are not studying him and his solution of the problem, but all of us colored people of whatsoever hue, are going to fight together for the general upbuilding of the Negro race, so that in the days to come we may be able to look back upon our effort with great pride, even as others worse positioned than ourselves have struggled upward to their present social, economic and political standing among races and nations. . . .

Is Du Bois Educated

DuBois seems to believe that the monopoly of education is acquired by being a graduate of Fisk, Harvard and Berlin. Education is not so much the school that one has passed through, but the use one makes of that which he has learned.

If DuBois' education fits him for no better service than being a lackey for good white people, then it were better that Negroes were not educated. DuBois forgets that the reason so much noise was made over him and his education was because he was among the first "experiments" made by white people on colored men along the lines of higher education. No one experimented with Marcus Garvey, so no one has to look upon him with surprise that he was able to master the classics and graduate from a university.

DuBois is a surprise and wonder to the good white people who experimented with him, but to us moderns he is just an ordinarily intelligent Negro, one of those who does not know what he wants.

The Man Who Lies

DuBois is such a liar when it comes to anything relating to the Universal Negro Improvement Association, the Black Star Line and Marcus Garvey that we will not consider his attacks on the Black Star Line seriously. He lied before in reference to this corporation and had to swallow his vomit. He has lied again, and we think a statement is quite enough to dispose of him in this matter.

This envious, narrow-minded man has tried in every way to surround the Universal Negro Improvement Association and Marcus Garvey with suspicion. He has been for a long time harping on the membership of the Universal Negro Improvement Association as to whether we have millions of members or thousands. He is interested because he wants to know whether these members are all paying dues or not, in that he will become very interested in the financial end of it, as there would be a lot of money available. DuBois does not know that whether the Universal Negro Improvement Association had money or not he wouldn't have the chance of laying his hands on it, in that there are very few "leaders" that we can trust with a dollar and get the proper change. This is the kind of leadership that the Universal Negro Improvement Association is about to destroy for the building up of that which is self-sacrificing; the kind of leadership that will not hate poor people because they are poor, as DuBois himself tells us he does, but a kind of leadership that will make itself poor and keep itself poor so as to be better able to interpret the poor in their desire for general uplift. He hates the poor. Now, what kind of a leader is he? Negroes are all poor black folk. They are not rich. They are not white; hence they are despised by the great professor. What do you think about this logic, this reasoning, professor? You have been to Berlin, Harvard and Fisk; you are educated and you have the "technique of civilization." . . .

Test of Education and Ability

When it comes to education and ability, Garvey would like to be fair to DuBois in every respect.

Suppose for the proof of the better education and ability Garvey and DuBois were to dismantle and put aside all they possess and were placed in the same environment to start life over afresh for the test of the better man? What would you say about this, doctor? Marcus Garvey is willing now because he is conceited enough to believe that in the space of two years he would make you look like a tramp in the competitive rivalry for a higher place in the social, economic world.

Let not our hearts be further troubled over DuBois, but let fifteen million Negroes of the United States of America and the millions of the West Indies, South and Central America and Africa work toward the glorious end of an emancipated race and a redeemed motherland.

Ignoring Freedom

DuBois cares not for an Empire for Negroes, but contents himself with being a secondary part of white civilization. We of the Universal Negro Improvement Association feel that the greatest service the Negro can render to the world and himself at this time is to make his independent contribution to civilization. For this the millions of members of the Universal Negro Improvement Association are working, and it is only a question of time when colored men and women everywhere will harken to the voice in the wilderness, even though a DuBois impugns the idea of Negro liberation.

9
Reactions to Du Bois' Programs for Self-Separation

*Du Bois' espousal of black self-separation and con-
certed all-black action met with a generally unfavorable response. One of the first black leaders to reply was Walter F.
White, the NAACP's executive secretary, who in 1934 outlined
that organization's reasons for committing itself to "the grim
struggle for integration and against segregation. . . ." A year
later, a controversial article appeared in* The Nation. *Entitled
"Black Chauvinism," its author was Benjamin Stolberg, who
contended that Du Bois, "having never developed an economic
philosophy, turned to black chauvinism. His latest battle cry
is that the Negro must recognize the curse of segregation and
build a black economy of his own. With what?" Stolberg
asked. "Is Wall Street colored? Is finance capital high yaller?
Today Du Bois winds up pretty much where Booker T.
Washington started. And so the colored people are leaderless."
Several letters, most of them critical, were written to* The
Nation *in response to Stolberg's article. But one was highly
favorable, describing the article as "a brilliant and sound
analysis of the tragic predicament of the American Negro
today." The authors of this letter were four brilliant black
scholars from Howard University: Sterling A. Brown, Ralph J.
Bunche, Emmett E. Dorsey, and E. Franklin Frazier. A few
months later, Frazier, a sociologist and the foremost scholar
of the black family, explained in greater detail his criticisms
of "The Du Bois Program in the Present Crisis."*

WALTER WHITE ON DU BOIS' PROGRAM [1]

Numerous requests have been made of the National Association for the Advancement of Colored People for a statement of the
position of the Association on editorials by Dr. Du Bois on "Segre-

[1] "Segregation—A Symposium," *The Crisis*, XLI (March 1934), 80–81.

gation" in . . . *The Crisis*. It is fitting and proper that the statement of the Secretary's position should first appear in *The Crisis*, the official organ of the Association.

Various interpretations have been placed upon Dr. Du Bois's editorial, a number of them erroneous and especially the one which interprets the editorial as a statement of the position of the N.A.A.C.P. The historic position of the N.A.A.C.P. has from the date of its foundation been opposed to segregation. Dr. Du Bois's editorial is merely a personal expression on his part that the whole question of segregation should be examined and discussed anew. There can be no objection to frank and free discussion on any subject and *The Crisis* is the last place where censorship or restriction of freedom of speech should be attempted. I wish to call attention to the fact that the N.A.A.C.P. has never officially budged in its general opposition to segregation. . . .

Let us put aside for the moment the ethical and moral principles involved. It is my firm conviction, based upon observation and experience, that the truest statement in the January editorial is:

> . . . there is no doubt that numbers of white people, perhaps the majority of Americans, stand ready to take the most distinct advantage of voluntary segregation and cooperation among colored people. Just as soon as they get a group of black folk segregated, they use it as a point of attack and discrimination.

. . . To accept the status of separateness, which almost invariably in the case of submerged, exploited and marginal groups means inferior accommodations and a distinctly inferior position in the national and communal life, means spiritual atrophy for the group segregated. When Negroes, Jews, Catholics or Nordic white Americans voluntarily choose to live or attend church or engage in social activity together, that is their affair and no one else's. But Negroes and all other groups must without compromise and without cessation oppose in every possible fashion any attempt to impose from without the establishment of pales and ghettoes. Arbitrary segregation of this sort means almost without exception that less money will be expended for adequate sewerage, water, police and fire protection and for the building of a healthful community. It is because of this that the N.A.A.C.P. has resolutely fought such segregation . . . ; has opposed restrictive covenants written into deeds of property, and all other forms, legal and illegal, to restrict the areas in which Negroes may buy or rent and occupy property.

This principle is especially vital where attempts are made to establish separate areas which are financed by moneys from the Federal or state governments for which black people are taxed at the same rate as white. No self-respecting Negro can afford to accept without vigorous protest any such attempt to put the stamp of Federal approval upon discrimination of this character. Though separate schools do exist in the South and though for the time being little can be done toward ending the expensive and wasteful dual educational system based upon caste and color prejudice, yet no Negro who respects himself and his race can accept these segregated systems without at least inward protest. . . .

It is admittedly a longer and more difficult road to full and unrestricted admission to schools, hospitals and other public institutions, but the mere difficulty of the road should not and will not serve as a deterrent to either Negro or white people who are mindful not only of present conditions but of those to which we aspire. In a world where time and space are being demolished by science it is no longer possible to create or imagine separate racial, national or other compartments of human thought and endeavor. The Negro must, without yielding, continue the grim struggle *for* integration and *against* segregation for his own physical, moral and spiritual well-being and for that of white America and of the world at large.

E. FRANKLIN FRAZIER ON DU BOIS' PROGRAM [2]

Since Emancipation, three outstanding Negro leaders have played the role of making articulate the changing phases of the Negro's philosophy of adjustment to American life. Frederick Douglass, who, prior to the Civil War, was a fiery anti-slavery orator, became the uncompromising defender of the Negro's right to full participation in American civilization. Just as Douglass died, Booker T. Washington rose to fame as the author of the formula for resolving the conflict between the whites and blacks in the South and as the hope of the disillusioned masses who had seen the concrete fruits of freedom snatched from them. But scarcely had Washington entered upon the stage with his preachments on thrift and

[2] "The Du Bois Program in the Present Crisis," *Race* (New York), I (1935–36), 11–13. Reprinted by permission of Mrs. Marie B. Frazier.

humility, when W. E. Burghardt DuBois, representing the educated Negro elite—or Talented Tenth as he called them—began his bitter attacks. With scathing pen and in brilliant style he tore the rags of hypocrisy from the northern white philanthropists who supported Washington; he castigated the savagery of southern poor whites and the hollow caste pretenses of the Bourbons. When Washington passed from the stage DuBois' philosophy was becoming more and more acceptable to the educated Negro both north and south, but Washington did not live to see his felicitously phrased platitudes falsified by the social and economic forces in American life.

On the other hand, DuBois has been denied the kindness of fate which his predecessors enjoyed. No outstanding successor has arisen to follow him on the stage of racial leadership. In fact, the scene has changed, and when DuBois attempts to act his former role his words become meaningless. Even when he attempts to say his own lines he often forgets them or gives a new version of his predecessor's or tries to anticipate the successor who should fit into the new scene. It is not difficult to discover why the role, which DuBois played in a masterly way because of his unique gifts and cultural background, cannot be fitted into the new social and economic scene. His role was one that derived its significance and character from that of his predecessor, Douglass, and his contemporary, Washington. All three of these leaders played upon a stage of racial leadership that took as its foundation the American economic and social system.

Marginal Man

However, the unique role which DuBois has played in American life can be understood only through a knowledge of the forces which molded his personality. He was born in New England, where his mulatto characteristics permitted him a large degree of participation in the life of the white world. During his short sojourn in the South as an undergraduate at Fisk University, where he was under New England white teachers, he never was thoroughly assimilated into Negro life. His return to New England afforded him a more congenial environment where he thoroughly absorbed the genteel intellectual tradition of Harvard. Two additional years in European universities made him a finished product of the aristocratic intellectual culture of the last decade of the nineteenth century.

But DuBois, aristocrat in bearing and in sympathies, was in fact a cultural hybrid or what sociologists have termed a "marginal man." Once back in America and in Atlanta, he was just a "nigger." Fine flower of western culture, he had here the same status as the crudest semi-barbarous Negro in the South. In the *Souls of Black Folk* we have a classic statement of the "marginal man" with his double consciousness: on the one hand highly sensitive to every slight concerning the Negro, and feeling on the other hand little kinship or real sympathy for the great mass of crude, uncouth black peasants with whom he was identified. For, in spite of the way in which DuBois has written concerning the masses, he has no real sympathetic understanding of them. *The Souls of Black Folk* is a masterly portrayal of DuBois' soul and not a real picture of the black masses. When he takes his pen to write of the black masses we are sure to get a dazzlingly romantic picture. Some one has remarked aptly that the Negroes in *The Quest of the Silver Fleece* are gypsies. The voice of DuBois is genuine only when he speaks as the representative of the Talented Tenth; for he is typical of the intellectuals who spring from oppressed minorities.

Romantic!

DuBois' program may be considered in its economic and social or cultural aspects. Perhaps it should be remarked in passing that there was no difference between the economic program of DuBois and that of Washington. Both envisioned the economic advancement of the Negro through thrift and intelligence. Whenever DuBois wrote of socialism, it was in a romantic vein. According to the recently released, seventh edition of the *Atlanta Creed*, socialism is a far-off, divine event toward which all creation moves. But, for the immediate economic salvation of the race he proposes that Negroes build "a co-operative industrial system in America, which to some extent will furnish employment, direct production and regulate consumption for gradually increasing numbers" of the Negro race. The Negro race is to "avoid the past errors of capitalism." This program, of course, is to be directed by the Talented Tenth who "refuse to remain parasites feeding on white philanthropy" and "welcome the burden of the uplift of our own masses until as a conscious and intelligent proletariat they can themselves assume democratic control of the whole group in the interest of our working class. Only in this way can the American Negro enter the new industrial kingdoms of the world, standing on his own economic feet."

The section of the program involving the encouragement of racialism should not occasion surprise. While it is true that only during recent years has DuBois advocated Negro schools and proposed that Negro colleges foster a racial culture, he has always displayed the typical racial consciousness of the cultural hybrid. While the Negro race is the same as any other, yet it has certain peculiar endowments. A statement by DuBois nearly a quarter of a century ago that the Negro was primarily an artist and that he had a characteristic "sense of beauty, particularly for sound and color" is a striking example of his romantic notions concerning the Negro's racial traits. In his recent program he would avoid "all artificial and hate-engendering deification of race separation as such" but would "just as sternly repudiate an enervating philosophy of Negro escape into an artificially privileged white race."

DuBois' racial program needs not to be taken seriously. Cultural hybrids often have "returned" to the minority race with which they were identified, glorified it and made significant additions to the artistic culture of the group. But DuBois remains an intellectual who toys with the idea of the Negro as a separate cultural group. He has only an occasional romantic interest in the Negro as a distinct race. Nothing would be more unendurable for him than to live within a Black Ghetto or within a black nation—unless perhaps he were king, and then probably he would attempt to unite the whites and blacks through marriage of the royal families. When Garvey attempted his genuine racial movement no one was more critical and contemptuous than DuBois of the fantastic glorification of the black race and all things black. Garvey's movement was too close to the black ignorant masses for DuBois. On the other hand, he was more at home with the colored intellectuals who gathered at the Pan-African congresses. If a fascist movement should develop in America, DuBois would play into the hands of its leaders through his program for the development of Negro racialism. As the situation is at present, the dominant social and economic forces in American life are destroying the possibility of the development of Negro nationalism.

Economically Impossible

The economic aspects of DuBois' program merit more serious consideration, since many educated Negroes who are groping for a solution of the race's economic problems may be deceived by the so-called practical nature of his program. Let us consider first his proposal that the Negro build a co-operative industrial system in America. When Garvey proposed a grandiose scheme for building a black commercial empire DuBois ridiculed his naïveté. But what could be more fantastic than his own program for a separate non-profit economy within American capitalism? Even if DuBois were ignorant of the mechanism of credit and the control of basic commodities by corporations, he must realize that consumers' co-operatives presuppose an income on the part of the consumers. With thousands of Negroes being displaced from the farms of the South while many more thousands are depending upon relief in the cities, a co-operative program could only adopt "Share Your Poverty" as a slogan. Even if Negroes, as DuBois implies, have an unusual endowment of altruism and will run businesses for service instead of profit, Negro consumers are going to buy where they can get goods at the cheapest price. To be effective on a large scale, co-operatives must compete with the modern corporation and there is no evidence that the Negro has the capital and skill to overcome this competition. Thus DuBois' co-operatives, which supposedly are a more practical approach to the solution of the Negro's economic plight than the alignment of black workers with economic radicals who can only offer salvation in the remote future, turn out to be fantastic. More than that, they set up false hopes for the Negro and keep him from getting a realistic conception of capitalist economy and the hopelessness of his position in such a system.

Since DuBois is an intellectual who loves to play with ideas but shuns reality, whether it be in the form of black masses or revolution, he likes to display a familiarity with Marxian ideology. In an article in the *Crisis* he demonstrated, in a few hundred words, the error of applying Marxian conceptions to the economic condition of the Negro in America. Later, in his *Black Reconstruction,* he played with Marxian terminology as a literary device. This is all as it should be, for DuBois has said that there shall be no revolution and that economic justice and the abolition of poverty shall come through reason (the intellectual speaks), sacrifice (the romanticist speaks), and the intelligent use of the ballot (in the end he remains a liberal).

The status of the race in America, which has been determined by those economic forces which have shaped the country at large, has remained unaffected by the programs of Negro leaders. Washington's program of industrial education and scientific farming offered no more salvation than Douglass' naïve faith that the Republican party was the ship and all else was the sea. Nor can DuBois, either as the intellectual or the romanticist, furnish the kind of social criticism which is needed today in order that the Negro may orient himself in the present state of American capitalism.

PART THREE

W. E. B. DU BOIS IN HISTORY

10

The Paradox of
W. E. B. Du Bois[1]

*One of the most insightful examinations of Du Bois'
thought and early actions is August Meier's "The Paradox of
W. E. B. Du Bois," which appeared as a chapter in Meier's
Negro Thought in America, 1880–1915 . . . (1963). It is in-
structive to compare Meier's analysis with the contemporary
analyses of Kelly Miller and John Spencer Bassett.*

If, of the great trio of Negro leaders, Frederick Douglass best
expressed the aspirations toward full citizenship and assimilation,
and Booker T. Washington the interest in economic advancement, it
was Du Bois who most explicitly revealed the impact of oppression
and of the American creed in creating ambivalent loyalties toward
race and nation in the minds of American Negroes. As Du Bois said
in 1897:

> One feels his two-ness—an American, a Negro, two souls, two
> thoughts, two unreconciled strivings, two warring ideals in one dark
> body. . . .
> The history of the American Negro is the history of this strife,—
> this longing to attain self-conscious manhood, to merge his double
> self into a better and truer self. . . . He would not Africanize
> America for America has too much to teach the world and Africa.
> He would not bleach the Negro soul in a flood of white American-

[1] August Meier, "The Paradox of W. E. B. Du Bois," in Meier's *Negro Thought
in America, 1880–1915: Racial Ideologies in the Age of Booker T. Washington*
(Ann Arbor: The University of Michigan Press, 1963), pp. 190–206. Reprinted
by permission of August Meier and The University of Michigan Press; footnotes
omitted with permission of the author. Copyright © 1963 by The University of
Michigan.

ism, for he knows that Negro blood has a message for the world. He simply wishes to make it possible for a man to be both a Negro and an American, without being cursed and spit upon. . . .

More than any other figure Du Bois made explicit this ambivalence —an ambivalence that is perhaps the central motif in his ideological biography. Even Du Bois has described himself as integrally a part of European civilization, and "yet, more significant, one of its rejected parts; one who expressed in life and action and made vocal to many, a single whirlpool of social entanglement and inner psychological paradox."

A proud and sensitive youth reared in a western Massachusetts town, Du Bois had occasion to know the sting of prejudice and early realized that "I was different from others; or like, mayhap in heart and life and longing, but shut out from their world by a vast veil." Subsequently he therefore found the segregated community of Fisk University, which he attended from 1885 to 1888, an enriching experience. Though he yearned for the full recognition of his American citizenship, he was also, he later recollected, "thrilled and moved to tears," and recognized "something inherently and deeply my own" as a result of his association there with a "closed racial group with rites and loyalties, with a history and a corporate future, with an art and a philosophy." By the time he received his A.B. from Fisk and entered Harvard as a Junior in 1888, "the theory of race separation was quite in my blood," and the lack of social acceptance he experienced at Harvard, he recalled later, did not disturb him. Yet it certainly was his sensitivity to discrimination that led him at this time to view Negroes as a "nation"—Americans, but rejected in the land of their birth.

Meanwhile, Du Bois had been expressing himself on other subjects. As a correspondent for Fortune's New York *Globe* during the early 1880's and as editor of the Fisk *Herald,* he displayed an interest in industriousness and ambition. Furthermore, as a student at Fisk and at Harvard—where he received his Ph.D. in 1895—and as a professor at Wilberforce University (1894–96), Du Bois proved more than willing to meet Southern whites half way. He told both Fisk students and his white associates in the Tennessee prohibitionist movement that the interests of the two races were essentially the same. To his Fisk audience he proposed the admittedly unorthodox idea that Negroes should divide their vote in order not to exacerbate race relations. He assured Southern whites that they could depend on the friendship of Negroes if only the whites would grant them citizenship rights and adequate educational facilities. Since the Negro's condition was such as to encourage prejudice, for their part Negroes must stress duties as well as rights, and work for their own advancement. At both Harvard and Wilberforce he could, in a single speech, lash out at America's immoral and un-American treatment of Negroes (and at Harvard suggest that Negroes would revolt if other means failed) and at the same time adopt a conciliatory position. Since Negroes had not yet achieved what it took the Anglo-Saxons a millennium to do, they were not yet equipped to vote. What he objected to was not the disfranchisement of the Negro masses, but of intelligent, law-abiding Negroes; and what he advocated was a franchise limitation fairly applied to both races along with adequate educational opportunities for all. In 1891 it was even reported in the *Age* that Du Bois had asserted that the whole idea underlying the Lodge Elections Bill was wrong, for it was proposed on the assumption that

> law can accomplish anything. . . . We must ever keep before us the fact that the South has some excuse for its present attitude. We must remember that a good many of our people . . . are not fit for the responsibility of republican government. When you have the right sort of black voters you will need no election laws. The battle of my people must be a moral one, not a legal or physical one.

It was no wonder then that after Washington's address Du Bois wrote the *Age* suggesting "that here might be the basis of a real settlement between whites and blacks."

Meanwhile, Du Bois was formulating his notion of leadership by a college-educated elite, which he regarded as necessary for the advancement of any group. In 1891 he deplored the South's effort to make common and industrial schools rather than colleges the basis of its educational system. For only a liberally educated white leadership could perceive that, despite the justification for overthrowing the Reconstruction governments, to permanently disfranchise the working class of a society in the process of rapid industrialization would, as socialists from Lassalle to Hindman had said, result in economic ruin. And only a liberal higher education could create an intelligent Negro leadership. Thus, while still a student at Harvard, Du Bois had suggested his theory of the talented tenth, foreshadowed his later concern with the working class, and adumbrated the

thesis he later stressed so much—that without political rights Negroes, primarily a working group, could not secure economic opportunity. Furthermore, it should be noted that his educational views
were not unrelated to his ethnocentric feelings. As he said at Wilberforce, the educated elite had a glorious opportunity to guide the
race by reshaping its own ideals in order to provide the masses with
appropriate goals and lift them to civilization.

After two years at Wilberforce, Du Bois accepted a one-year research appointment at the University of Pennsylvania. Then in 1897
he became professor of sociology at Atlanta University, where he
remained until 1910, teaching and editing the annual Atlanta University Studies on the American Negro.

At no time in his life did Du Bois place greater and more consistent stress upon self-help and racial solidarity than during the last
four years of the century. Like many of his contemporaries he fused
this emphasis with one on economic advancement; and like a few
of them he synthesized it with his educational program for the
talented tenth. To Du Bois in fact, the race prejudice which isolated
the Negro group and threw upon it "the responsibility of evolving
its own methods and organs of civilization" made the stimulation
of group co-operation "the central serious problem."

It was his appointment to the University of Pennsylvania that pro-
vided Du Bois with his first opportunity to begin a scientific study
of the race problem. He had long awaited such an opportunity because he believed that presentation of the facts derived from scientific investigation would go a long way toward solving the race problem. The resulting monograph, *The Philadelphia Negro*, leaned
toward the blame-the-Negro, self-help point of view. Yet Du Bois
did describe what it meant to be snubbed in employment and in
social intercourse, and he judged that the Negro's participation in
politics had been, in net effect, beneficial to the city and to the
Negro himself. Above all, he felt that Negroes must uplift themselves, and by racial co-operation open enterprises that would provide employment and training in trades and commerce. Whites had
their duty to help but society had too many problems "for it lightly
to shoulder all the burdens of a less advanced people." Negroes
ought to constantly register strong protests against prejudice and injustice, but they should do so because these things hindered them in
their own attempt to elevate the race. And this attempt, Du Bois
held, must be marked by vigorous and persistent efforts directed

toward lessening crime and toward inculcating self-respect, the dignity of labor, and the virtues of truth, honesty, and charity.

Like Washington, then, Du Bois combined an enthusiasm for racial solidarity with one for economic development and the middle-class virtues. In fact, he regarded a college education as "one of the best preparations for a broad business life" and for the making of "captains of industry." Likening Negroes to other nationalities, he chided them for being ashamed of themselves, and held that such success as had been achieved by other nations no larger in population than the American Negroes could be accomplished only through a badly needed co-operation and unity. In view of the poverty of the Negro and the economic spirit of the age, it was most important to achieve success in business. Because of race prejudice the major opportunity for such achievement lay in commercial activity based on Negroes pooling their earnings and pushing forward as a group. Though their collective capital be small, thrift and industry could succeed even under the handicaps of prejudice. Under the circumstances a penny savings bank would be more helpful than the vote. Negroes should patronize and invest their money in Negro-owned enterprises, even at a personal sacrifice. For "we must cooperate or we are lost. Ten million people who join in intelligent self-help can never be long ignored or mistreated."

It should be noted, of course, that Du Bois did not, during the *fin de siècle* years, give up all interest in political rights, though like the majority of articulate Southern Negroes of the day he was willing to compromise on the matter. He was among those who in 1899 petitioned the Georgia legislature not to pass the Hardwick disfranchisement bill, though like Booker T. Washington he was willing to accept an educational and/or property qualification as long as free school facilities were open to all.

During this period Du Bois was more emphatic than at any other time about the value of racial integrity. Speaking on "The Conservation of Races" in 1897 he asserted that there existed subtle psychic differences, which had definitely divided men into races. Like his racist contemporaries, he was certain of the universality of "the race spirit," which he regarded as "the greatest invention for human progress." Each race had a special ideal—the English individualism, the German philosophy and science, and so forth. Therefore, "only Negroes bound and welded together, Negroes inspired by one vast ideal, can work out in its fullness the great message we have for humanity." To those who argued that their only hope lay in amalgamating with the rest of the American population, he admitted that Negroes faced a "puzzling dilemma." Every thoughtful Negro had at some time asked himself whether he was an American, or a Negro, or if he could be both; whether by striving as a Negro he was not perpetuating the very gulf that divided the two races, or whether Negroes "have in America a distinct mission as a race." Du Bois' answer was what is now called cultural pluralism. Negroes were American by birth, in language, in political ideas, and in religion. But any further than this, their Americanism did not go. Since they had given America its only native music and folk stories, "its only touch of pathos and humor amid its mad money-getting plutocracy," it was the Negroes' duty to maintain "our physical power, our intellectual endowment, our spiritual ideas; as a race, we must strive by race organizations, by race solidarity, by race unity to the realization of the broader humanity which freely recognizes differences in men, but sternly deprecates inequalities in their opportunity of development." To this end, separate racial educational, business, and cultural institutions were necessary. Despised and oppressed, the Negroes' only means of advancement was a belief in their own great destiny. No people that wished to be something other than itself "ever wrote its name in history; it must be inspired with the Divine faith of our black mothers, that out of the blood and dust of battles will march a victorious host, a mighty nation, a peculiar people, to speak to the nations of the earth a Divine truth that should make them free." Washington, it should be pointed out, while advocating race pride and race integrity, did not glory so much in the idea of a distinctive Negro culture (though he was always proud of the spirituals or "plantation melodies"). Nor did he exhibit Du Bois' sense of identification with Africans, evident in Du Bois' advocacy of "pan-Negroism" in this same address.

During the last years of the century Du Bois developed his educational theories at considerable length, attempting to construct "A Rational System of Negro Education" by reconciling the two widely diverging tendencies of the day—training for making a living and training for living a broad life. All agreed, he said, on the necessity of universal common school training, and on the contribution Hampton, Tuskegee, and the Slater Fund had made in stressing the building of an economic foundation, the freedmen's primary concern. But unfortunately only three or four schools made broad culture their chief aim. Du Bois criticized the talk of rosewood pianos in dingy cabins, of ignorant farmers, of college graduates without employment, though he agreed that more stress had been placed on college training than the economic condition of the race warranted. But the vogue for industrial education had become so great that the colleges were hard-pressed for funds. This was particularly deplorable because the isolation of the Negro community demanded the creation of an indigenous leadership of college-trained captains of industry and scholars, who would advance the masses economically and culturally, and who could view the race problem from a broad perspective.

There were remarkable similarities between Du Bois and Washington during the late 1890's—a period when more Negro leaders than at any other time adopted a conciliatory tactic. Both tended to blame Negroes largely for their condition, and both placed more emphasis on self-help and duties than on rights. Both placed economic advancement before universal manhood suffrage, and both were willing to accept franchise restrictions based not on race but on education and/or property qualifications equitably applied. Both stressed racial solidarity and economic co-operation. Du Bois was, however, more outspoken about injustices, and he differed sharply with Washington in his espousal of the cause of higher education.

The years from 1901 to 1903 were years of transition in Du Bois' philosophy, years in which he grew more critical of industrial education and more alarmed over disfranchisement. Writing in 1901 he engaged in sharp protest against the Southern race system, even while recognizing that Negroes must adjust to it. He denied that the "many delicate differences in race psychology" excused oppression. He complained of the economic discrimination that retarded the development of a substantial landowning and artisan class. He bemoaned the lack of contact between the races that increased prejudice by preventing the best classes of both races from knowing each other. Yet he felt that, since Negroes must accept segregation, the road to uplift and economic improvement lay in the development of college-educated leaders: "Black captains of industry and missionaries of culture" who with their knowledge of modern civilization could uplift Negro communities "by forms of precept and example, deep sympathy and the inspiration of common kindred and ideals." But while Negroes would have to temporarily acquiesce in segregation, they could not acquiesce in disfranchisement. Du Bois did not object to "legitimate efforts to purge the ballot of ignorance, pauperism and crime," and he conceded that it was "sometimes best that a partially developed people should be ruled by the best of their stronger and better neighbors for their own good," until they were ready to stand on their own feet. But since the dominant opinion of the South openly asserted that the purpose of the disfranchisement laws was the complete exclusion of Negroes from politics, the ballot was absolutely necessary for the Negro's safety and welfare. Moreover, as European experience had demonstrated, workers under modern industrial conditions needed the vote in order to protect themselves; Negroes, laboring under racial discrimination, needed it even more.

Du Bois developed further his educational views and the theme of the talented tenth. He agreed that it was most important to train Negroes to work, and he conceded that industrial schools would play an important role in achieving this end. He also approved of the compromise function of industrial education, which had brought together races and sections; and although industrial education would not solve the problem he asserted that "it does mean that its settlement can be auspiciously begun." Yet he had come to criticize the overinsistence of industrial schools upon the practical, the unfortunate opposition of their advocates toward colleges, the fact that industrial schools were preparing their students in obsolete crafts, and the fact that they produced few actual artisans. Du Bois defended Negro colleges from charges that they had erred in training school teachers and professional men before turning to industrial training. He pointed out that historically the European university had preceded the common school, and that out of the liberal arts institutions came the backbone of the teaching force of the Negro common schools and of industrial schools like Tuskegee, where almost half of the executive council and a majority of the heads of departments were college graduates. All races, he held, had been civilized by their exceptional men; "the problem of education, then, among Negroes, must first of all deal with the Talented Tenth."

It is evident that Washington and Du Bois had come to disagree not only in their educational philosophy, but also on the fundamental question of the immediate importance of the ballot. By 1903 Du Bois was not only pleading for higher education, but had begun to criticize the work of the industrial schools. Both men spoke of captains of industry, but where the Tuskegeean emphasized economic skills, the Atlanta educator stressed a high grade of culture. And unlike Washington, Du Bois had come to believe that educational and property qualifications for voting would not be equitably applied. True, Du Bois never gave up his belief that, in the face of white prejudice and discrimination group solidarity was necessary, especially in economic matters. But all that really remained to make the two men irreconcilable ideological opponents was for Du Bois to advocate the importance of protest rather than accommodation. This he did in his opening attack on Washington in 1903.

During the 1890's Washington and Du Bois had been cordial in their relationships. Upon returning to the United States from Germany in 1894 Du Bois accepted a position at Wilberforce, having had to turn down a somewhat later offer from Tuskegee. Again in 1896, 1899, and as late as 1902 Du Bois seriously considered invitations to Tuskegee. In his correspondence with Washington, through his articles and speeches, and by attending the Hampton and Tuskegee Conferences he exhibited his sympathetic interest in Washington's work. He had, it is true, mildly criticized the Tuskegeean in an article in 1901. In it he said that some of the most prominent men of the race regarded the Hampton-Tuskegee approach as only a partial approach to the race problem, in that they stressed the highest aspirations of the race, advocated college education, and believed that Negroes should enjoy suffrage equally with whites. But as late as July 1902 the *Guardian* denounced Du Bois for siding with Washington at the St. Paul meeting of the Afro-American Council. "Like all the others who are trying to get into the bandwagon of the Tuskegeean, he is no longer to be relied upon," declared the editor, Monroe Trotter.

Kelly Miller has asserted that Trotter wove a "subtle net" around Du Bois and captured him for the radical cause. It would be difficult to test the truth of this statement. Certain it is, however, that by January 1903 Trotter was praising Du Bois as a brilliant leader who, despite temptations, "has never in public utterance or in written article, betrayed his race in its contest for equal opportunity and equal rights." Du Bois himself has recalled that he was gradually growing more disturbed after 1900—less by the ideological difference between him and Washington (which he remembered as mainly one of emphasis) than by the immense power over political appointments, over philanthropic largess, and over the press wielded by what Du Bois has labeled the "Tuskegee Machine." Du Bois found Washington's influence over the press especially deplorable, in view of the Tuskegeean's soft-pedaling of agitation on segregation and disfranchisement. Yet whatever his actual motivation for criticizing Washington, his first public statement on the matter was confined to ideological issues.

This statement was Du Bois' famous essay, "Of Booker T. Washington and Others," in *Souls of Black Folk,* published in the spring of 1903. "Easily the most striking thing," began Du Bois, "in the history of the American Negro since 1876 is the ascendancy of Mr. Booker T. Washington." Others had failed in establishing a compromise between the North, the South, and the Negroes. But Washington, coming with a simple though not entirely original program of industrial education, conciliation of the South, and acceptance of disfranchisement and segregation, had succeeded. For with "singular insight" he had grasped the spirit of the age—"the spirit and thought of triumphant commercialism."

Du Bois went on to criticize the Tuskegeean because his policy "practically accepted the alleged inferiority of the Negro," allowed economic concerns to dominate over the higher aims of life, and preached a "submission to prejudice." Although Washington had made some statements about lynching and the franchise, generally his speeches purveyed the "dangerous half-truths" that the Negro's lowly condition justified the South's attitude and that the Negro's elevation must depend chiefly on his own efforts. Du Bois perceived paradoxes in Washington's attempt to make Negro workers businessmen and property owners when it was impossible for workers to defend themselves without the ballot; in his preaching self-respect while counseling accommodation to discrimination and in his advocacy of industrial and common schools while depreciating the colleges that supplied their teachers. Furthermore, Washington's propaganda had undoubtedly hastened the disfranchisement, the increased segregation, and the decreased philanthropic concern for higher education that accompanied his ascendancy.

Washington's popularity with whites, Du Bois held, had led Negroes to accept his leadership, and criticism of the Tuskegeean had disappeared. The time was ripe therefore for thinking Negroes to undertake their responsibility to the masses by speaking out. In addition to the few who dared to openly oppose Washington, Du Bois thought that men like Archibald and Francis J. Grimké, Kelly Miller, and J. W. E. Bowen could not remain silent much longer. Such men honored Washington for his conciliatory attitude, and they realized that the condition of the masses of the race was responsible for much of the discrimination against it. But they also knew that prejudice was more often a cause than a result of the Negro's degradation; that justice could not be achieved through "indiscriminate flattery"; that Negroes could not gain their rights by voluntarily throwing them away, or obtain respect by constantly belittling themselves; and that, on the contrary, Negroes must speak out constantly against oppression and discrimination.

Du Bois had indeed moved away from his conciliatory ideology of the 1890's. Yet attempts at co-operation between him and Washington were not quite at an end. In the summer of 1903 Du Bois spoke at Tuskegee. The two men also continued their collaboration —begun in 1902—in an effort to prevent the exclusion of Negroes from Pullman cars. Nevertheless, after the "Boston Riot" Du Bois was—with reservations—lining up with Trotter. He did not, he said, agree with Trotter's intemperate tactics, but he admired his integrity and purpose, which were especially needed in view of Washington's backward steps. The Carnegie Hall Meeting of January 1904 and Du Bois' appointment to the Committee of Twelve temporarily restored an uneasy working relationship between him and Washington, but he soon resigned from the Committee and in 1905 was chiefly responsible for inaugurating the Niagara Movement. Meanwhile, he has recollected, he found it increasingly difficult to obtain funds for his work at Atlanta, experienced criticism in the Negro press, and in other ways "felt the implacability of the Tuskegee Machine." He was one of the most active members of the Conference on the Negro in 1909, and when the N.A.A.C.P. was organized in 1910 he became director of publicity and research and editor of the *Crisis*.

Thus by 1905 Du Bois had definitely come to the parting of the ways with Washington. And it is in the Niagara Movement manifestoes and in the pages of the *Horizon* and *Crisis* that one can best observe Du Bois as the consistent agitator, the ardent and brilliant fighter for integration and citizenship rights. For example, he insisted that disfranchisement retarded the economic development of the Negro because the voteless could not protect their property rights. He cited cases of persecution of prosperous Negroes as evidence that Washington's program would not obtain the respect of the white man and the rights of citizenship. In a typical editorial he pointed out that in spite of Washington's conciliatory policy conditions had grown worse. True, as Washington said, Negroes had continued to accumulate property and education, but how Washington could assert that discrimination and prejudice were decreasing was incomprehensible to Du Bois. Horrible as race prejudice was, it could be fought if faced frankly. But "if we continually dodge and cloud the issue, and say the half truth because the whole stings and shames . . . we invite catastrophe." Elsewhere he insisted that opportunism was a dangerous policy that gave moral support to the race's enemies, and he denounced the stress on sycophancy, selfishness, mediocrity, and servility at the expense of the best education, the highest ideals, and self-respect. Naturally he criticized industrial schools. On one occasion he attacked Hampton for its opposition to the work of the Negro colleges, and described it as "a center of that underground and silent intrigue which is determined to perpetuate the American Negro as a docile peasant," lacking political rights and social status. Du Bois was unequivocal in his stand on segregation. He scathingly denounced the separate-but-equal doctrine: "Separate schools for Whites and Blacks, and separate cars for Whites and Blacks are not equal, can not be made equal, and . . . are not intended to be equal." He charged that what the South wanted was not mere separation but subordination, and insisted that no "square deal" was possible as long as segregation existed. And unlike Washington he opposed a colored Episcopal bishop to work only among Negroes, even though this would have elevated a Negro to a high church office.

It is evident from a reading of Du Bois' less publicized scholarly and nonpolemical statements that throughout these years he still maintained his interest in racial solidarity and self-help, in the group economy, and in the American Negro's ties to Africa. On occasion he was most explicit about his concept of economic nationalism. Just as a country can by tariffs build up its separate economy to the point where it can compete in international trade, so the Negro should create a group economy that would "so break the force of race prejudice that his right and ability to enter the national economy are assured." His enthusiasm for the group economy was indeed at times interpreted as implying a favorable attitude toward segregation, and in an exchange of letters on the subject with the editor of the Boston *Transcript,* Du Bois was finally prompted to declare that while opposed to physical separation he was prepared to accept for some time to come a "spiritual" separation in economic life that would involve Negroes trading only among themselves. True, he shifted his support from the creation of captains of industry who would exploit the Negro proletariat to the building up of a consumers' and producers' co-operative movement among Negroes.

But inevitably he had to reconcile his espousal of a group economy with his demands for full integration. In 1913, replying to a communication which claimed it was hard to meet the argument that segregation forced Negroes to develop themselves, Du Bois agreed that undoubtedly thousands of Negro businesses, including the *Crisis,* had developed because of discrimination, capitalizing, in a sense, on race prejudice. But this did not make discrimination a "veiled blessing." While Negro enterprises had done creditable work under the circumstances, and although Negroes must make the best of segregation, turning even its disadvantages to their advantage, they "must never forget that none of its possible advantages can offset its miserable evils, or replace the opportunity . . . of free men in a free world."

A similar paradox was involved in Du Bois' stand on intermarriage. Writing in the *Independent* in 1910 he held that a person had the right to choose his spouse, that the prohibition of intermarriage was not justified when it arbitrarily limited friendships, and that where satisfactory conditions prevailed, race mixture had often produced gifted and desirable stocks and individuals, such as the Egyptians, and Hamilton, Pushkin, Douglass, and Dumas. He believed, however, that for the present widespread intermarriage would be "a social calamity by reason of the wide cultural, ethical and traditional differences" between the races, and predicted that if Negroes were accorded their rights and thus encouraged to build up their racial self-respect, the two races would continue to exist as distinct entities, perhaps forever, and this not "at the behest of any one race which recently arrogantly assumed the heritage of the earth, but for the highest upbuilding of all peoples in their great ideal of human brotherhood."

Nor was Du Bois consistent in his views on race differences. Earlier, while never accepting any idea of Negro inferiority, he had referred to Negroes as a backward, childlike, undeveloped race, and he had accepted the idea of inherent racial differences. But in March 1908 he attacked the "glib" Darwinist interpretations about undeveloped races and the survival of the fittest. After the Universal Races Congress in London in 1911 Du Bois enthusiastically reported its conclusion that there was no proven connection between race and mental or cultural characteristics. Yet in 1913 he harked back to the idea of inherent racial differences and described the Negro as primarily an artist, possessing a "sensuous nature . . . the only race which has held at bay the life destroying forces of the tropics,"

gaining thereby an unusual aesthetic sensitivity. This quality explained the artistic achievements of the Egyptians and the Ommiads,
the literature of Pushkin, the bronze work of Benin, and the "only
real American music."

As a matter of fact Du Bois maintained his strong feeling of identification with other colored peoples, especially Africans. At one
time he was secretary of a company which aimed to participate in
the economic advancement of East Africa. Years before Melville J.
Herskovits cited anthropological evidence for African origins of
the culture of American Negroes, Du Bois held that their religious
life and institutions, family life, burial and beneficial societies, the
roots of economic co-operation, and the skill of Negro artisans all
had their origins in Africa. Finally, *The Negro,* published in 1915,
dealt with Negro history from ancient Egypt to the United States
and was especially notable for its discussion of the history and culture of West Africa. In it he also adopted the Italian anthropologist
Giuseppe Sergi's thesis that an ancient rather dark-skinned race
spawned all of the ancient Mediterranean civilizations. Moreover,
he predicted the emergence of a pan-African movement, uniting
Negroes everywhere, and a growing unity of the darker races against
the intolerable treatment accorded them by the white man. Since
the colored races were in a majority, the future world would probably be what colored men make it, and "in the character of the
Negro race is the best and greatest hope. For in its normal condition it is at once the strongest and gentlest of the races of men."

A new theme in the pages of the *Horizon* and *Crisis* was Du Bois'
interest in the labor movement and in socialism. At one time he
had viewed the white working class as the Negro's "bitterest opponent." By 1904 he had come to believe that economic discrimination was in large part the cause of the race problem, and to feel
sympathetic toward the socialist movement. Three years later, he
was writing favorably of the socialists in the *Horizon.* Elsewhere he
advised the socialists that their movement could not succeed unless
it included the Negro workers, and wrote that it was simply a matter
of time before white and black workers would see their common
economic cause against the exploiting capitalists. Though in 1908
Du Bois did not vote for the socialists because they had no chance
of winning, in 1911 he joined the party. In a Marxist exegesis in the
concluding pages of *The Negro,* Du Bois viewed both American
Negroes and Africans, both the white workers and the colored races,
as exploited by white capital which employed the notion of race

differences as a rationalization of exploitation, segregation, and subordination. And he predicted that the exploited of all races would
unite and overthrow white capital, their common oppressor.

Du Bois' espousal of the cause of labor was so deep-seated that he
had the *Crisis* printed by members of a union that did not admit
Negroes, and in its pages he welcomed the rare signs that white and
Negro workers might be getting together. In this regard he was
certainly ahead of his time, and even he finally expressed discourage-
ment after the 1917 East St. Louis riot in which white unionists
played such a striking role. Thus Du Bois' attempts to woo union
labor had succeeded no better than his related attempt to woo the
Democratic party. . . . But Du Bois never gave up his vision of a
union of white and black workers creating a society of economic and
racial justice. He had in fact shifted from pinning his faith on the
intellectuals or talented tenth of professional and business men to
pinning it on the actions of the black working classes, though quite
likely they were to be led, as has been suggested, by a talented-tenth
intelligentsia.

In W. E. B. Du Bois then, the most distinguished Negro intellectual in the age of Booker T. Washington, we find explicitly stated
most of the threads of Negro thought at that time. On the one hand
he had a mystic sense of race and of the mission of the Negro, which
made him sympathetic toward ideas of racial pride and solidarity
as sentiments useful for racial uplift. On the other hand he held explicitly and constantly, especially after 1901, to the ideal of waging
a struggle for full acceptance in American society. While at times
he seemed to view segregated institutions as good in themselves, actually he regarded them as second-best instruments in the struggle
for advancement and citizenship rights. He envisaged not amalgamation but cultural pluralism as the goal. He was inconsistent on the
question of innate race differences, but he never admitted that Negroes were inferior. Above all he insisted that Negroes wanted to be
both Negroes and Americans, maintaining their racial integrity
while associating on the freest terms with all American citizens, par-
ticipating in American culture in its broadest sense, and contributing
to it in fullest freedom.

It is notable that though Du Bois expressed the views held by
most of the articulate Negroes of the age of Booker T. Washington,
both in his stress on racial solidarity and economic co-operation and
in his demand for full citizenship rights, nevertheless he frequently
found himself in the minority. Few articulate Negroes exhibited the

same extent of political independence; not many Northern Negroes agreed with his accommodating tactic of the late nineteenth century; relatively few championed the cause of liberal education as enthusiastically as he did; few either dared or cared to follow him in the extent to which he championed the protest movement during the first years of the twentieth century; and few embraced socialism or the cause of the black workers and interracial working-class solidarity. It is important to note, however, that many times people, who at heart agreed with his point of view, were not courageous enough to flout the power structure both within and outside of the Negro community as he did.

Of the great trio of Negro leaders, Douglass was the orator, Du Bois the polished writer, and Washington the practical man of affairs. Like Douglass, Du Bois has been known primarily as a protest leader, though he was not as consistent in this role as Douglass. Like Douglass, too, he exhibited a marked oscillation in his ideologies—in fact his was more marked than that of Douglass. Like Douglass he clearly stated the ultimate goals which Washington obscured. Yet Du Bois displayed more of a sense of racial solidarity than Douglass usually did. Nor did he envisage the degree of amalgamation and the loss of racial consciousness that Douglass regarded as the *summum bonum*. On the contrary he, like Washington, emphasized race pride and solidarity and economic chauvinism, though after 1905 he no longer championed support of the individualist entrepreneur but favored instead a co-operative economy. Where Washington wanted to make Negroes entrepreneurs and captains of industry in accordance with the American economic dream (a dream shared with less emphasis by Douglass), Du Bois stressed the role of the college-educated elite and later developed a vision of a world largely dominated by the colored races which would combine with the white workers in overthrowing the domination of white capital and thus secure social justice under socialism. All three emphasized the moral values in American culture and the necessity of justice for the Negro if the promise of American life were to be fulfilled. But of the three men it was Douglass who was pre-eminently the moralist, while Washington and Du Bois expressed sharply divergent economic interpretations. Where Douglass and Washington were primarily petit-bourgeois in their outlook, Du Bois played the role of the Marxist intelligentsia. Where the interest of Douglass and Washington in Africa was largely perfunctory, Du Bois exhibited a deep sense of racial identity with Africans. Above all, though only Douglass favored amalgamation, all three had as their goal the integration of Negroes into American society.

Scholar and prophet; mystic and materialist; ardent agitator for political rights and propagandist for economic co-operation; one who espoused an economic interpretation of politics and yet emphasized the necessity of political rights for economic advancement; one who denounced segregation and called for integration into American society in accordance with the principles of human brotherhood and the ideals of democracy, and at the same time one who favored the maintenance of racial solidarity and integrity and a feeling of identity with Negroes elsewhere in the world; an equalitarian who apparently believed in innate racial differences; a Marxist who was fundamentally a middle-class intellectual, Du Bois becomes the epitome of the paradoxes in American Negro thought. In fact, despite his early tendencies toward an accommodating viewpoint, and despite his strong sense of race solidarity and integrity, Du Bois expressed more effectively than any of his contemporaries the protest tendency in Negro thought, and the desire for citizenship rights and integration into American society.

11

Du Bois: Tragic Figure or Prophet?

The following two evaluations of Du Bois are obviously at odds with each other. Francis L. Broderick, author of W. E. B. Du Bois: Negro Leader in a Time of Crisis *(1959), has argued that the closing three decades of Du Bois' life were years of relative isolation from the civil rights movement to which he had devoted his intellect, energy, and soul. According to Broderick, two turning points distinguished his later years. First of all, his "plan" for "self-separation" in 1934 "ended Du Bois' career as a leader of his race." Secondly, his Cold War estrangement from the United States and attachment to the Soviet Union heightened his isolation not only from civil rights but even from his own race. "Because Negro leaders refused to copy his enthusiasm for the Soviet Union," Broderick has written, "because Negro leaders generally failed to heed and to succor him, he publicly turned his back on their efforts." Du Bois' legacy will always be crucial to America's black people, Broderick concludes, but the final decades of his life were years of discontinuity, anticlimax, and, ultimately, of tragedy.*

Truman Nelson's article is in strong disagreement. To Nelson, Du Bois was a "prophet" whose political journey from the NAACP to the Communist Party and residency in Africa was not only logical but, in view of the witchhunting of the McCarthy era, essential. The tragedy was not Du Bois', Nelson asserts, it was America's. "When," Nelson has asked, "will the people learn to cherish their prophets, to defend them with their lives, to let them be heard, to make them be heard?"

DU BOIS: TRAGIC FIGURE? [1]

W. E. B. DuBois is a lonely and tragic Negro. Once a national audience, black and white, heard his plea for Negro equality. Now

[1] Francis L. Broderick, "The Tragedy of W. E. B. Du Bois," *The Progressive,* XXII (February 1958), 29–32. Reprinted by permission of *The Progressive.*

few listen, and fewer still heed him. Once Negro leaders looked to him as the patron saint of their struggle. Now he . . . embarrasses them.

When the Supreme Court handed down its desegregation decision in the spring of 1954, who thought to say that the modern movement for Negro rights, of which the Court's decision was a momentary climax, owed more to DuBois than to any other single man? Negroes are looking for equality by 1963, the hundredth anniversary of the Emancipation Proclamation. When DuBois set that goal sixty years before, black Americans were still moving in a dark night of discrimination—segregation, disfranchisement, lynching—with the darkest hours still ahead. For more than thirty years he prodded the white man's conscience and the Negro's courage. Then he broke with the forces for civil rights and with his own great past just as the struggle was about to register real gains. Chasing after a pipe dream of Negro separatism, he found himself far from the battlefield when his side started winning, and when he finally did return, there was no room for him in the top command. Even so, he could have been—indeed was for a few years—venerated as the Negro's elder statesman. But he lost this role too when he preached the Soviet Union's version of socialism and peace. Now few remember him, and of the few, part remember only his pro-Soviet posture.

DuBois matured in the world of Booker T. Washington, whose speech at the Atlanta Exposition in 1895 was a landmark in Negro history. There Washington offered the white South an attractive deal—in exchange for economic opportunity, that is, industrial education and jobs, the Negro would put off his insistence on political, civil, and social rights. Though Washington never explicitly disclaimed a single Negro right, his accommodating, diplomatic words made white Southerners think they could deal with the Negro on their own terms. His program was designed to soothe racial tensions by allaying white apprehension of aggressive Negro demands, by guaranteeing a stable Negro labor force in the South, and bargaining for security and education for the Negro.

As a result of the "Atlanta compromise," Washington became the Negro's unofficial ambassador to white America, and his prestige in the white world, particularly among politicians and philanthropists, gave him almost regal status in the Negro world until his death in 1915.

Though originally friendly to Washington's position, DuBois soon joined up with a group of noisy dissenters—mainly northern,

urban, educated Negroes—who charged that Washington was selling
out the Negro's heritage as a man and as an American for a mess of
economic pottage. A mulatto of French Huguenot, Dutch, and
Negro ancestry, DuBois—the name is pronounced Du-Boyce—had
grown up in Great Barrington, Massachusetts, and had been educated at Fisk, Harvard, and Berlin. After jobs at Wilberforce and
at the University of Pennsylvania, he had gone to Atlanta University
as a professor of sociology, a pioneer in collecting data on Negro life.

Behind his conflict with Washington was the clash of two dis-
cordant personalities. Both possessed titanic ambition. Washington,
thick set and slow moving, had the confidence of a self-trained man.
A shrewd, calculating judge of people, he had the soft speech and
the accommodating manner which made him equally at home among
sharecroppers and at the President's table. A master of equivocation,
he could make platitudes pass as earthly wisdom, and he could take
back unnoticed with one hand what he had given with the other.
Slight and nervous in his movements, DuBois never for a moment
forgot his educational background. Arrogant and outspoken, he
held aloof from the Negro masses, but felt at home with a small
company of his peers, with whom he could be witty and convivial.
Washington had the appearance of a sturdy farmer in his Sunday
best; DuBois, with a well-trimmed goatee, looked like a Spanish
aristocrat. Where Washington was accommodating, DuBois was
fretful and aggressive. The conflict between them became official in
1903 when DuBois published an attack on Washington in his most
famous book, *The Souls of Black Folk.* Seven years later he left
Atlanta to join white progressives like Oswald Garrison Villard to
set up the National Association for the Advancement of Colored
People (NAACP).

The NAACP, a sort of Twentieth Century abolitionist society,
concentrated on civil and political rights, using civil suits, organized
protest, and education as its weapons. DuBois, editor of the NAACP's
magazine, *The Crisis,* supported these activities, yet at the same time
he was impatient with the Association's merely negative program
of fighting obstructions. He wanted the Negro to plan the development of his own group through building and loan associations, co-
operatives, even a Negro party (though this last was muted).

Through the *Crisis* and the Association and through an annual
nationwide lecture tour, DuBois' voice became the loudest in the
race. Washington's death in 1915 removed the great rival, and no

one took Washington's place. What's more, the Negro was leaving the farm, and more important, he was moving North in substantial numbers: in the decade from 1910 to 1920, Chicago's Negroes more than doubled, and Detroit's multiplied seven times. For this group Washington's views no longer had meaning, and they were ready to hear the more uncompromising DuBois. Gathered in Northern urban ghettos, they had strength of numbers and the right to vote, powerful weapons in their own defense. These conditions worked in DuBois' favor. The *Crisis* and the Association gave him a spring-board to power, for in the Negro world he became the symbol of their work. Executive officers of the NAACP, white men all until 1920, came and went, and none ever made his will felt as an inde-pendent force. As a result, local branches of the NAACP all over the nation identified the work of the Association with the vigorous editor whose views the members—70,000 by 1919—received every month. Behind the *Crisis* and the Association, they saw a single figure—the austere, uncompromising, scholarly Dr. DuBois, unapproachable and unafraid.

By the end of the decade, DuBois reached his pinnacle. The year after Washington's death, Negro leaders of all views and all sections arrived unanimously at a statement of policy not measurably differ-ent from DuBois' views. After America's entry into the war, Negro leaders gathered in Washington to promise support of the war, but also to insist on the training of Negro officers, an end to lynching, universal suffrage, universal and free common school training, abolition of the Jim Crow car, repeal of segregation ordinances, equal civil rights in public institutions. At both meetings DuBois' program spoke the mind of the articulate race leaders.

To be sure, DuBois never inherited Washington's authority; no Negro did. DuBois' voice carried further than any other single Negro's, but it never rang with command; it was more like the loudest voice in a large and dissonant chorus. Furthermore, within the range of his influence DuBois handicapped himself by righteous, tempestuous arrogance. He could get away with this tone with many Negroes; but when he complained about the incompetence of the Negro press and the rascality of Negro clergymen, he was needling his most important potential allies. The less educated elements of the Negro population might put up with DuBois' arrogance as the price of his intellectual greatness. But men of comparable intelli-gence and training—Professor Alain Locke of Howard University was a Rhodes scholar—were not ready to accept DuBois' view of

himself at its face value. Yet with all these reservations, the essential
fact remains that no other Negro in 1920 reached a national audience
so effectively.

For fifteen more years DuBois stayed on with the NAACP as
editor of his almost personal magazine, the *Crisis*. His goal remained
the same—full rights for all Negro Americans immediately. But
the war had chilled his expectations from white America. Progres-
sivism had let the Negro down, and when the Negro returned from
the Great Crusade, he was met by the "Red Summer" of 1919 which,
according to John Hope Franklin, "ushered in the greatest period
of interracial strife the nation had ever witnessed." For an angry
moment, DuBois recommended violence as the answer to violence.
Then when anger burned itself out almost as completely as the
idealism of the war years, he settled down to a long struggle.

Since white America, even liberal white America, had done so
little for the Negro, DuBois looked about for new allies. He found
two possibilities: dark-skinned men everywhere in the world who
were growing restive under their white colonial masters, and the
Russian revolutionists. The one led to the Pan-African movement,
the other to a steady enthusiasm for the Soviet Union.

The Pan-African movement took the form of a series of congresses
at which colored men representing no one but themselves gathered
in Europe to condemn white colonialism. They accomplished little
beyond forcing DuBois to do some fresh thinking about colonial
problems.

The Soviet Union was a more rewarding enthusiasm, for socialism,
as DuBois saw it, gave voice to the depressed masses, black and
white. Initially cautious, he soon pronounced Russia "the most
amazing and hopeful phenomenon" in the post-war world, and after
a subsidized trip to Russia in 1926, he told his *Crisis* readers: "I
stand in astonishment and wonder at the revelation of Russia that
has come to me. I may be deceived and half-informed. But if what
I have seen with my own eyes and heard with my own ears is
Bolshevism, I am a Bolshevik." Like Pan-Africa, Russia seemed to
offer a glimpse of the future, especially because of its "workingman's
psychology" and its freedom from a color line. Negatively, it gained
by the hatred of those white powers which bore the special brunt of
DuBois' disapproval.

Yet the paragon existed at a distance, and DuBois' enthusiasm for
Russia did not extend to American Communists, the "young jack-

asses" who mouthed Marxist cliches without understanding American conditions. The sentiment was reciprocated: the Communists labeled DuBois an imperialist follower of Booker T. Washington, a "betrayer of the Negro people" and a spokesman for "Negro bourgeois reformism." In this context DuBois' enthusiasm for Russia had no domestic effects.

The Great Depression created a new situation. Long the victim of a tradition of "last hired, first fired," the Negro suffered out of proportion to his numbers as the economy slid downward. Ever conscious of his responsibility as the race's leader—he never doubted it even when others did—DuBois searched for a way out. White America had done little, even in prosperous years; Pan-Africa was dead for the moment; world socialism was remote, and domestic socialism, Communist or non-Communist, promised the Negro nothing. His people facing disaster, he turned to the only allies on whom he felt the Negro could count: his twelve million Negro fellow Americans. He told his people to look for economic security in voluntary segregation—the formation of a Negro economy within the American economy. Let Negroes work for their own people, using their purchasing power to support their own. Their universities could plan for them, their businessmen could organize, their artists could enrich. Let white men flounder in capitalist greed; the Negro could flourish in cooperative sufficiency. Segregation without discrimination, he called it.

The plan ended DuBois' career as a leader of the race. To the NAACP, with which he had been associated for the 24 years since its beginning, segregation, however veiled, was anathema, and the organization let him go. The Negro and his white friends had worked with the old DuBois, uncompromising fighter for full equality, too long to turn to a new DuBois who sounded like Booker T. Washington. His old programs frustrated, his new plan rejected, DuBois went back to Atlanta University, as alone as he had been in his undergraduate days at Harvard.

A decade passed at Atlanta, with a good deal of homage to an old man no longer at the center of power; honorary degrees from Atlanta, Fisk, and Wilberforce; a testimonial 70th birthday party; membership in the National Institute of Arts and Letters. He wrote a weekly newspaper column, published a book, founded *Phylon*, a sociological quarterly, and organized regional conferences of Negro land-grant colleges. People forgot about his plan for Negro self-sufficiency; he all but forgot it himself. The older generation paid him the respect due to a great pioneer; the younger generation rarely heard his name. Then in 1944 his contract at Atlanta was abruptly terminated, and he returned to New York and to the NAACP for another round of controversy.

DuBois' return to the arena created difficulties. He was easier to venerate than to work with, and Negro leaders ready to canonize him as the patron saint of Negro equality were not ready to surrender power to him. Back at the Association's offices, where once he had thundered, his role was narrowed to post-war colonial policy and "special research," while other hands—to DuBois, cold hands —wove the fibers of policy. Walter White, with whom DuBois had feuded bitterly before the break in 1934, was now in charge. White was a gregarious, nimble, talented negotiator who used first-name diplomacy to expand Negro opportunity. For four years tensions about administration taxed the patience of both sides. How much office space was the Elder Statesman to have? Who was to open the mail? The two communicated through memoranda. When they met in an elevator the size of a large broom closet, they managed not to see each other. Policy divided them even more decisively. Despite endless denials, White was friendly to the Truman Administration, this at a time when DuBois thought that President Truman was supporting colonial powers at the expense of subject peoples and was looking for a capitalist war to crush Russia. When these views led DuBois to support Henry A. Wallace publicly in 1948, White used the occasion to have DuBois fired.

For DuBois the pattern of the post-war world was clear: England and the United States were imperialist and discriminatory, Russia was neither. Business interests controlled America's direction: the Baruch plan was a trick to prevent the peacetime use of atomic energy; the Truman Doctrine armed Greece against Russia for the benefit of Great Britain; the Marshall Plan promised large profits to American investors and sought to re-establish European wealth at the expense of the colonies. On the other hand, no tarnish dulled the luster of the Soviet Union: Molotov was "the one statesman at San Francisco who stood up for human rights and the emancipation of colonies." The clarity of this balance gave order in a complex world.

American Communists and others similarly well disposed to Russian policy welcomed their new ally. Forgotten were the epithets on both sides. DuBois was wooed with vigor. The *New Masses* published his articles, gave him an award, named him a contributing editor. When he was dismissed from the Association, *Masses and Mainstream* and the *Daily Worker* screamed condemnation. Later on he became "one of the greatest living Americans," and finally the "recognized 'Dean of American Letters.'" For his part, DuBois said he would be a "fellow traveler with Communist or capitalist, with white man or black," as long as "he walks toward the truth."

DuBois had a remarkably busy career with his new friends. After his dismissal from the Association, he joined the Council on African Affairs as vice-chairman. . . . Then he mounted the "peace" crusade as a featured speaker: New York in March 1949, Paris in April, Moscow in August, and Prague the following year. He became chairman of the Peace Information Center in New York City, the American agency for collecting signatures to the "Stockholm peace petition." In the fall of 1950, he ran for the U.S. Senate against Herbert H. Lehman and Joe R. Hanley on the American Labor Party ticket. Then in February 1951, a Washington grand jury indicted DuBois and others for failing to register the Peace Information Center as the "agent of a foreign principal."

The indictment marked the final turning point in DuBois' career. When the case came to trial, the presiding judge dismissed it because the government failed to establish a nexus between DuBois' group and any foreign principal. Yet as a result of the trial, DuBois cut himself loose from the American struggle for equality and associated himself with a "world concept of human uplift," the forces fighting for peace and for the working classes. In DuBois' view these forces were best represented by Russia. Mulling over the post-war world and his own trial, sorting out friends and enemies, he charged that colored leaders all over the world had abandoned their people to become lackeys of capitalism. Ralph J. Bunche, who had won the Nobel Peace Prize for achieving a truce between Israel and the Arab states, had made the Negro an unwitting partner to the betrayal of democracy in Israel when he should have "stood firm against vacillation, compromise, and betrayal by our Department of State." Negroes had moved far in fifty years—they could move no farther unless they fought American capitalist-imperialists hell-bent on curbing social welfare and destroying Russia. On essential points—peace, socialism, education, race prejudice—Russia, in DuBois' view, had no peer. The United States could expect his loyalty, but Russia won his hopes. Because Negro leaders refused to copy his enthusiasm for the Soviet Union, because Negroes generally failed to heed and to succor him, he publicly turned his back on their efforts.

The final break put a tragic end to DuBois' career, for the Negro in America owes him much. One cannot say that the Negro's progress since 1903 is the result of DuBois' agitation: DuBois' ideas belonged to others as well, and many forces other than agitation have contributed to the Negro's advance in fifty years. Yet DuBois, more than anyone else, pointed the way for the Negro by his steady refusal to allow the Negro comfort in anything less than his full rights as an American. Hammering away at America's conscience and at the Negro's pride, arguing, cajoling, threatening, retreating when necessary, advancing when possible, he staked out the Negro's claim so unmistakably that others could carry on when he faltered. At home, and abroad as well, in South Africa as well as in the United States, his writings gave colored men courage for their fight. His monthly editorials held up the strong, re-charged the wavering, and flayed the compromisers. The *Crisis* became the record of Negro achievement; its columns gave recognition to success in every field, and young artists could find there a place for their creations. Even Du Bois' aloofness became an asset—it removed him in Negro eyes from everyday life and, by giving him a transcendent quality, it raised the goal of aspiration. The austere Dr. DuBois reminded Negro intellectuals that courage and talent could carry a man—and a race—far. . . .

OR DU BOIS: PROPHET? [1]

In the beginning the prophet sees pre-conditions, the explosive present and the transcendental future like a man sitting by the window of a darkened room, reading by strokes of lightning. A flash of insight, of foreboding, flares across his consciousness, and then he is plunged back into the confusions and the doubts of the ordinary mortal, groping his way through what may always be a total darkness and incomprehension of his private world and his fate in it. In time the flashes come closer and closer until the world he is destined to illumine lights up under his hand with an incandescent glare and he is able to hold its crimes and secrets, its dungeons and despairs, to a steady cleansing glow which crackles and consumes like a forest fire.

---

[1] Truman Nelson, "W. E. B. Du Bois As a Prophet," *Freedomways*, V, No. 1 (Winter 1965), 47–58. Reprinted by permission of *Freedomways* magazine.

The world of W. E. B. Du Bois was the world of color, and its people the majority of all the earth's people. I think of him as WORLD MAN ONE. No man ever moved within a wider bracket of humanity. Early in his life he "made it" with the whites; there were no intellectual prizes nor artistic achievements that he could not have taken from them at will, if he had chosen . . . chosen to be the "exception" whites are reluctantly willing to thrust upward to prove that they are "democratic." He did not want this, ever. Not only because it was morally wrong, and DuBois was one of the most consistent moralists of all time, but because it was a false notion. The whites permit "exceptions" because they think of themselves with complacent blindness as the majority, and thus quite safe from being overturned by a handful of alien, inexplicable men of genius from outside, or *below,* where they usually place them.

What a searing lightning bolt W. E. B. Du Bois launched against this false, jerry-built elevation back in 1911. "The coming world man is colored. For the handful of whites in this world to dream that they, with their presently declining birthrate, can ever inherit the earth and hold the darker millions in perpetual subjection is the wildest of wild dreams." But it was a successful dream the whites had, because, as in a dream, they could choose their own landscape and the people in it, and as they moved on in the cataleptic trance of their own skin, they kept always just outside the penumbra of their consciousness, so as to be invisible, the "dark race" and the "dark Continent" from which they came. . . .

Du Bois changed all this. After reading him the black presence invades the whole consciousness. Grandeurs of intellect, perception, revolutionary thrust and power become apparent. And so does that ideology of lies which props up those centuries of white "liberalism" in which everything is judged by the words, by its "sentiments" and never by its fruits. In which "liberty and justice for all" means liberty and justice for *some* . . . of the white people, by the white people and for the white people. In which all our talk about the perfectability of a man and with the perfectability of *me* . . . the white, superior me, first, and the black man can wait for the half loaf, or the crumbs, or whatever is left over as "time" settles this vexing problem. . . .

No one knew better than he the great potential of the black race. His profound historical sense (for the prophet is an historian above all else) drove him to find the evidence to reverse the whole historical canon, deliberately falsified, which pictured the Reconstruction period as proving that the Negro was not competent to rule himself. After the Civil War, "Industry gave the black freedmen the vote, expecting them to fail, but meantime to break the power of the planters. The Negroes did not fail; they enfranchised their white fellow workers, established public schools for all and began a modern socialistic legislation for hospitals, prisons and land distribution. Immediately the former slave owners made a deal with the Northern industrial leaders for the disenfranchisement of the freedmen . . . the freedmen lost the right to vote, but retained their schools, poorly supported as they were by their own meager wages and Northern philanthropy."

"Northern philanthropy," by controlling the money bags, forced upon the Negro a failure of nerve, convincing their leader, Booker T. Washington, that all was lost and that the Negro school and college had to be used as a saving remnant . . . and these schools to be mainly work-training schools. Washington and his lieutenants began to retreat and to even cringe before the white avalanche of ridicule and abuse which swept away, or buried their will to resist. Du Bois could not contain his anger at this. He did what every prophet must do at some time or other, turn on his own people when they are wrong, when they are suicidal. With the cruelty of the light beam of a doctor's exploration of some putrid sore in the secret membranes, he showed them what they were becoming by not resisting at all levels the pressures of reaction.

He was a master at rediscovering and correctly analysing the hidden continuities between events and trends which seem to have no surface connection. Booker T. Washington's retreat into proving the Negro's case by his ability to "work hard and save," his tactic of trying to shrink a great race into a mere petty bourgeoisie while they were still standing and struggling as *men,* did just what Du Bois predicted it would—brought on increasing spirals of suppression and degradation, coming full circle after the election of Woodrow Wilson, in the re-segregation of the Capitol itself, and culminating, in the country, with a foul wave of lynching, terror and newly enacted racist law, nearly as bad as in slavery times.

Du Bois wanted them to fight, every day, for everything the white man had, right across the board. He called for an education that was a real education, not mere job training, and those jobs of the menial sort. Work was not education—education was the development of power and ideal—the source of art, of understanding. Work was too often to the Negro only a way of being used. He wanted black boys and girls to storm the heights held by Beethoven and Rembrandt, by Shakespeare and Pasteur. Why not? Du Bois was no diplomat, he drove a hard truth. Nor was he a pacifist; nor did he ever want to shed "our" blood before "theirs."

"Let no one," said Du Bois in 1913, "for a moment mistake that the present increased attack on the Negro along all lines is but the legitimate fruit of that long campaign for subserviency and surrender which a large party of Negroes have fathered now some twenty years . . . only the blind and foolish can fail to see that a continued campaign in every nook and corner of this land, preaching to white and colored, that the Negro is chiefly to blame for his condition, that he must not insist on his rights, that he should not take part in politics, that Jim Crowism is defensible, and even advantageous, that he should humbly bow to the storm until the lordly white man grants him clemency—the fruit of this disgraceful doctrine is disenfranchisement, segregation, lynching. Fellow Negroes, is it not time to be men? Is it not time to strike back when we are struck? Is it not high time to hold up our heads and clench our teeth and swear by the Eternal God we will *not* be slaves and that no aider, abettor, and teacher of slavery in any shape or guise can longer lead us?"

In 1913 and 1914 Du Bois' flashes of revelation began to fuse and stay lit and the pages of *The Crisis* for these years are one great coruscating glare. No wonder, said Du Bois, the sly Mister Dooley said the black man was "aisily lynched," they had made themselves the mudsills for the western world; when their wives were called prostitutes and their children bastards, they smiled; when they were called inferior half-beasts, "We nodded our simple heads and whispered, 'we is.'" When they were accused of laziness, they shrieked "ain't it so." They laughed at jokes about their color, about their tragic past and their compulsions to steal chickens. And what was the result? asked the prophet. " 'We got *friends!*' I do not believe any people ever had so many 'friends' as the American Negro today. He has nothing but 'friends' and may the good God deliver him from most of them, for they are like to lynch his soul."

Then came World War One and his great soul was torn from the plight of his own people to the suffering of the world. He had to think now of all men. He went to Europe. . . . "Fellow blacks," he said, "We must join the democracy of Europe," for there he found the dirty race hatred of America did not exist. He became aware of the Russian Revolution: that it was the one saving remnant of the bloody war. He went to the Soviet and said, "If what I have seen with my own eyes and heard with my own ears in Russia is Bolshevism, I am a Bolshevik!" Coming back to the United States he was in an agony of soul over what it did to his people, seen clearly from distant shores. *"It lynches . . . it disfranchises its own citizens . . . it encourages ignorance . . . it steals from us . . . it insults us . . . and* it looks upon any attempt to question or even discuss this dogma as arrogance, unwarranted assumption and treason." . . .

He realized with the ultimate political sophistication that all workers were disenfranchised in respect to the wealth and power they create and felt that the workers should determine the policies of all public services through owning them themselves. There was no question about him being a socialist; . . . but when he looked around him and saw, over and over again, the black man being excluded from trades or held down to the lowest grade of job, and heard on the other hand, the radical parties extolling the organized Union as the vanguard of the revolutionary class, he cried out in anger and frustration, "Black brother, how would you welcome a dictatorship of this proletariat?"

It is a sign of the true prophet that although he cries out in the wilderness and into the unheeding voice of the whirlwind, he wants to gain the hearts and minds of all men . . . he wants to join the millions: he is not in the least exclusive. Over and over again, by pleading, by flogging, by toil and example of the very highest order, Du Bois tried to lead his people into the promised land of equality and fulfillment. He created a Negro intelligentsia, poets and exhorters who sometimes equalled and occasionally surpassed him in their denunciation and awarenesses of their white oppressors.

Obviously there was no majority for them here on American soil, but in the world, and particularly in Africa, there was a spiritual majority which could buoy them up and sustain them as they moved their frail, despised twenty million souls against the towering mass of white indifference and actual oppression. Du Bois tried to make them feel the confidence of being in a majority. "Most men in this world are colored. A faith in humanity, therefore, a belief in the gradual growth and perfectibility of men must, if honest, be primarily a belief in colored men." But where could he demonstrate this perfectibility? Where but in the home place, the motherland! His prophet's instinct told him that Africa could be the great base for the transformation of black people everywhere.

He brought this presence to black Africa's table, scraped bare and gouged and splintered by white imperialist greed and looting. First, in 1900, there was a "Pan African Conference" in London, called by a West Indian. There were only thirty people there, among them Du Bois, and it had no roots in Africa itself, but it was a beginning. Then, after the Allied victory in World War I, hearing the pious disclaimers of the victors that they wanted, not blood and loot, but only "self-determination for all nations," Du Bois went to Paris to ask Wilson why he could not begin with the self-determination of the African colonies held by the defeated Germany. This is the way of the prophet; he demands the transformation of flowery words into solid fruit.

This idea was greeted with official indifference and in the press with scornful laughter. "An Ethiopian Utopia, to be fashioned of the German colonies, is the latest dream of the Negro race . . . Dr. Du Bois's dream is that the Peace Conference could form an internationalized Africa, to have as its basis, the former German colonies, with their 1,000,000 square miles and 12,500,000 population . . . to this, his plan reads, could be added by negotiation, Portuguese and Belgian Africa . . . within ten years, 20,000,000 black children ought to be at school. . . ." (Chicago *Tribune,* January, 1919).

Du Bois organized a congress around this idea, to sit simultaneously with the Versailles Conference, enlightening and rebuking it, showing it the way to real peace, with an example of the nonexploitation of people. . . .

This was "Utopia" for the white world. Well, you can hardly blame them for this . . . they haven't made it; obviously the natives of this land of the free have not effective ownership of their own land, they have no "higher" technical or cultural education that is *free,* the state does not protect them in the least, from the exploitation of Capital and investments . . . nor is it ever possible, under present conditions, for anyone but a millionaire, or the hired creature of a billion dollar corporation, to "extend" his political participation to the "higher offices of state."

This ideological base was fortified and armed, again and again, by African Congresses coming in 1921, in 1923, in 1927, coming to a climax in 1945. Much of the expenses of these congresses were paid for out of Du Bois' pockets, although he had to subsist on the meager earnings of a scholar and editor.

Someone else is telling the story of the African revolution and his part in it, but it is part of the making of a prophet to record all his triumphs and failures, and by the stupendous irony of time, just at the moment when Kwame Nkrumah heard first the locks open on his prison door, and walked then into the office of the alien Governor of his occupied country, to hear, then, himself asked to form the first free government his country had known since their enslavement by imperialist England, Du Bois heard the clank of an American prison door, opening to close him in.

The time had come when he had to face his mob. It was the whole country, it was the government, the courts, the press, the Congress, the F.B.I., the State Department, the Justice Department, all bearing down on him with a malignancy that would seem insane, except that motives had at the core, the central truth that he, with his wisdom and prophecy, was threatening their overthrow. That lynch mob of the rotten center which goes by the name of "law and order" and "security," had decided that because he had been on a committee to achieve nuclear disarmament in a world on the brink of self-extinction, that he was an agent of a foreign power and subject to a fine of ten thousand dollars and five years in jail.

When he heard of his indictment in February of 1951, he was aghast at the presumption, at the disgrace. . . . He felt that this was the utter rending of the fabric of his work; that all his achievements were blotted out as he stood, as the government's lynch mob made him stand, in open court with handcuffs on his wrist, when they put him into a medieval cage with human derelicts, when they fingerprinted him, searched him for concealed weapons and performed all the other barbarous acts of insult that people, presumed to be innocent before trial, have to endure when they fall into the hands of the police.

His arraignment took place in February, 1951, his trial in November. . . . For a long while he could not wholly understand why this was happening to him: he knew he was innocent, he had never taken, never seen any money or support for his committee from a foreign power. But then between the hammer and the anvil of the process experience, he began to renew, in its final essence, the revolutionary impulse that went deep in the marrow of his life.

He realized that he was on trial as a criminal because he had been the most prominent American in the circulation of the Stockholm Appeal, which said, "We consider that the first government henceforth to use the atomic weapon against any country whatsoever will be committing a crime against humanity and should be treated as a war criminal." He did not know, but he might have sensed, that the U.S. Government was meditating the use of atomic weapons against the people of Korea, people of color like himself. As the war went on and the immorality of American policy in Asia became clearer he realized why he, although other people were on trial with him, was singled out as the real culprit and why it was always said of him, in the newspapers, that he was a Negro. He felt that his persecutor's "real object was to prevent American citizens (particularly those of the Negro race) of any sort, from daring to think or talk against the determination of big business to reduce Asia to colonial subserviency to American industry, to reweld the chains on Africa, to consolidate U.S. control of the Caribbean and South America; and above all to crush Socialism in the Soviet Union and China. That was the object of this case."

More and more he became conscious that this was a war against people of another color, akin to his own, and that his towering presence as a Negro nuclear pacifist was extremely embarrassing to a government using Negro troops against other colored people. . . . "Worst of all" [said Du Bois] "is the use of American Negro troops in Korea. Not only is this bound to leave a legacy of hate between the yellow nations and the black, but the effect on Negroes of America, in a sense compelled to murder colored folks who suffer from the same race prejudice that they do at home, to be dumb tools of business corporations, this is bound to result in the exacerbation of prejudice and inner conflict here in America."

His defense cost him $35,150, and it was all for nothing; the case was dismissed after some days of trial, without ever going to the jury. The government had no case, said the judge. And the protests from countries all over the world who saw the condemned man as a giant among dwarfs, bore down on a nervous and uneasy State Department. So his only punishment for his innocence and truth was six months and more of agony as an indicted criminal, begging literally for his life . . . for who stays long in jail, or in life, at the age of 83? The state was wrong, but who punishes them? "A nation steals and destroys, yet no individual is guilty, no one is to blame, no one can be punished."

After his trial, after the establishment of his innocence, he was still tainted in the eyes of the rotten center, the lynch mob. The soaring crescendoes of the African liberation movement exploded like fireworks. White pundits from Minnesota, from Walla Walla, from everywhere and anywhere but Africa, came in droves to TV

and radio to "explain" the African revolutions. Across the river
from the tower on the Empire State Building lived the man who
had prophesied it and helped make it. Nobody asked him; nobody
put in a ten-cent phone call to have him explain it. Now he was in
exile. America acted as if he did not exist. Great countries outside
wanted him for their honored guest; a few colleges dared listen to
him briefly, but all that dammed-up wisdom and experience had no
outlet into the mainstream of American life.

This was the final tragedy. The prophet silenced: isolated by
petty defamation, by suspicion, by officially contrived alienation.
Oh the waste of this! His country wasted him as some great natural
resource is wasted; like a mountain wasted for a carload of ore, a
forest splintered to make newsprint for the publication of trivia
and lies. Wasted as Frederick Douglass and Garrison were wasted;
Nat Turner and John Brown. Du Bois could have been greater than
any of these, if only by the sheer longevity of his presence amongst
us. If only because he embodied in his person the whole process
experience of the American Negro from the time he was freed until
now . . . and in his intellectuality and integrity, in his selflessness
and lack of race chauvinism, gave to his own people a sense of their
own attainable human grandeur, and to the whites an inescapable
reminder of their racial shamelessness. When will the people learn
to cherish their prophets, to defend them with their lives, to let
them be heard, to *make* them be heard? When will they realize that
wasting them like this means in due time, the tragic waste of themselves, or their sons sometimes, perhaps always, on bloody battle
fields where their young blood and promise runs out into the
unremembering earth!

The small, nobly erect and intact figure began to bend a little
from weariness and pain. This enforced silence was for him, a
damned defeat. But then he had his final triumph . . . greater than
Moses, greater than all the prophets. There are few moments in
history more moving than when Kwame Nkrumah, in all the erect-
ness and power of a young manhood that had wrested a new nation
from a continent thought to be eternally dark and despised, and
filled it with effusions of light, came to the old man and said, "Father, we want you to come home."

And so the great prophet returned to the land of his ancestors,
to walk its bustling streets, full of the buoyancy of people living a
life of revolutionary promise and advance, seeing in the faces of

passers-by the reflected glory of his presence. He died there, and the cold sea rolls between us now. He was my great man and I miss him, but the indestructible terrain of his life and work, his writing and prophecy unites me with him, and transmits his warmth, as the stony bed of the ocean valley carries warmth and unites Africa to these troubled shores.

Bibliographical Note

In his sixty years of writing for publication, W.E.B. Du Bois compiled a massive bibliography. Beginning as a teenager (see P. G. Partington, "The Contributions of W.E.B. Du Bois to the New York 'Globe,' and the New York 'Freeman,' 1883–1885," *Negro History Bulletin*, XXXIII [February 1970]), Du Bois continued to write until his death in 1963. His major books are listed by date of publication in the preceding "Chronology of the Life and Major Works of W.E.B. Du Bois." Many of his writings are frankly autobiographical; the most significant of these are portions of *The Souls of Black Folk* (1903); *Darkwater: Voices from Within the Veil* (1920); *A Pageant in Seven Decades, 1868–1938* (1938); *Dusk of Dawn: An Essay toward an Autobiography of a Race Concept* (1940); "My Evolving Program for Negro Freedom," in Rayford W. Logan, ed., *What the Negro Wants* (1944); *In Battle for Peace: The Story of my 83rd Birthday* (1952); and *The Autobiography of W.E.B. Du Bois . . .* (1968). A Du Bois autobiography is also available in record form: "W.E.B. Du Bois— a Recorded Autobiography" (Folkways Records, 1961).

In recent years, due to a marked resurgence of interest in Du Bois and his ideas, there has been a proliferation of anthologies of his writings. Among the most comprehensive and perceptive of these are: Philip S. Foner, ed., *W.E.B. Du Bois Speaks: Speeches and Addresses, 1890–1963*, two volumes (1970); Julius Lester, ed., *The Seventh Son: The Thought and Writings of W.E.B. Du Bois*, two volumes (1971); Henry Lee Moon, ed., *The Emerging Thought of W.E.B. Du Bois: Essays and Editorials from The Crisis . . .* (1972); Andrew G. Paschal, ed., *A W.E.B. Du Bois Reader* (1971); Meyer Weinberg, ed., *W.E.B. Du Bois: A Reader* (1970); and Walter Wilson, ed., *The Selected Writings of W.E.B. Du Bois* (1970). There are also several biographies of Du Bois, as well as two collections of articles appraising his life, thought, and accomplishments. Two excellent scholarly biographies by historians are: Francis L. Broderick, *W.E.B. Du Bois: Negro Leader in a Time of Crisis* (1959); and Elliott M. Rudwick, *W.E.B. Du Bois: Propagandist of the Negro Protest* (1960). Other biographies are: Shirley Graham Du Bois, *His Day Is Marching On: A Memoir of W.E.B. Du Bois* (1971); Leslie Alexander Lacy, *The Life of W.E.B. Du Bois: Cheer the Lonesome Traveler* (1970); Emma Gelders Sterne, *His Was the Voice: The Life of W.E.B. Du Bois* (1971); and a book for younger readers: Dorothy Sterling and Benjamin Quarles, *Lift Every Voice: The Lives of Booker T. Washington, W.E.B. Du Bois, Mary Church Terrell, and James Weldon Johnson* (1965). The two anthologies appraising Du Bois' accomplishments are valuable, for they not only contain the documented studies of historians and other scholars, but each also has a helpful bibliography. Rayford W. Logan, a longtime colleague and friend of Du Bois, has compiled ten scholarly essays in *W.E.B. Du Bois: A Profile* (1971). The other anthology was assembled by the editors of *Freedomways*. Entitled *Black Titan: W.E.B. Du Bois* (1970), this book is an expanded version of that magazine's Du Bois Memorial Issue (*Freedomways*, V [Winter 1965]). A significant feature of *Black Titan* is Ernest Kaiser's "A Selected Bibliography of the Published Writings of W.E.B. Du Bois." Some of the other books mentioned above also contain excellent bibliographies of writings by and about Du Bois; among them are Rudwick's biography, the collections edited by Lester, Weinberg, and Wilson, and, in *The Autobiography of W.E.B. Du Bois . . .* (1968), a bibliography compiled by Herbert Aptheker. Superficial but still useful is another bibliography: S. I. A. Kotei, comp., *Dr. W.E.B. Du Bois 1868–1963: A Bibliography* (1964).

Du Bois has been the subject of numerous articles. Many contemporaries, for example, wrote about the Du Bois-Washington controversy; see John Spencer Bassett, "Two Negro Leaders," *South Atlantic Quarterly*, II (July 1903); Kelly Miller, "Radicals and Conservatives," in his *Race Adjustment: Essays on the Negro in America* (1909); and William H. Ferris, Chapter XLVIII in *The African Abroad, or His Evolution in Western Civilization, Tracing His Development under the Caucasian Milieu*, Vol. II (1913). Among the most perceptive historical evaluations of the controversy are the Rudwick and Broderick biographies and August Meier's outstanding study, *Negro Thought in America, 1880–1915: Racial Ideologies in the Age of Booker T. Washington* (1963). One of the first people to try to describe the personality and daily life of Du Bois was John Henry Adams, in "Rough Sketches: William Edward Burghardt Du Bois, Ph.D.," *Voice of the Negro*, II (March 1905). As perhaps the most influential Afro-American ideologist of the twentieth century, Du Bois was prominently discussed in magazine articles about "the Negro Problem," black leadership in America, and "the New Negro." Some of these articles are: Horace M. Bond, "Negro Leadership since Washington," *South Atlantic Quarterly*, XXIV (April 1925); V. F. Calverton, "The New Negro," *Current History*, XXIII (February 1926); E. Franklin Frazier, "The American Negro's New Leaders," *Current History*, XXVIII (April 1928); S. Graham, "Militancy of Colour and Its Leaders," *19th Century and After*, LXXXVIII (November 1920); Abram L. Harris, "The Negro Problem as Viewed by Negro Leaders," *Current History*, XVIII (June 1923); and Guy B. Johnson, "Negro Racial Movements and Leadership in the United States," *American Journal of Sociology*, XLIII (July 1937). See also the chapters on Du Bois in B. Brawley, *Negro Builders and Heroes* (1937); and Mary White Ovington, *Portraits in Color* (1927). The decade of the 1930's was one of travail for Du Bois, primarily because of the opposition to his programs of "voluntary self-segregation" and the all-black "cooperative commonwealth." For anal-

yses of this conflict, see issues of *The Crisis* for 1934; James Weldon Johnson, *Negro Americans, What Now?* (1935); E. Franklin Frazier, "The
Du Bois Program in the Present Crisis," *Race,* I (1935–36); Benjamin
Stolberg, "Black Chauvinism," *The Nation,* CXL (May 15, 1935), and the
letters written in reply to this article; and Raymond Wolters, "W.E.B.
Du Bois and the Depression: Self-Help and Economic Recovery," in Wolters' *Negroes and the Great Depression* . . . (1970). From the 1940's to
the mid-1960's, writers generally saw much to criticize and little to praise
in Du Bois' current programs and ideological commitments; a sample of
these articles would include: Francis L. Broderick, "The Tragedy of
W.E.B. Du Bois," *Progressive,* XXII (February 1958); William Gorman,
"W.E.B. Du Bois and His Work," *Fourth International,* II (May–June
1950); Ralph McGill, "W.E.B. Du Bois," *Atlantic Monthly,* CCXVI
(November 1965); and George Streator, "A Negro Scholar," *The Common-
weal,* XXXIV (May 2, 1941). Exceptions to this observation are: Lerone
Bennett, Jr., "W.E.B. Du Bois: Prophet of Protest and Pan-Africa,"
Ebony, XX (March 1965); W. S. Braithwaite, "A Tribute to W.E.
Burghardt Du Bois . . . ," *Phylon,* X (4th Quarter 1949); Robert Morss
Lovett, "Du Bois," *Phylon,* II (3rd Quarter 1941); and Truman Nelson,
"W.E.B. Du Bois: Prophet in Limbo," *The Nation,* CLXXXVI (January
25, 1958). In recent years praise has generally replaced criticism. One
occasion for this praise was the 1968 publication of *The Autobiography,* for
this gave reviewers an opportunity to reassess Du Bois' life and work.
Some of the most significant of these reviews are: Martin Duberman,
"Du Bois as Prophet," *New Republic,* CLVIII (March 23, 1968); Truman
Nelson, "A Life Style of Conscience," *The Nation,* CCVI (April 29, 1968);
and Gilbert Osofsky, "Master of the Grand Vision," *Saturday Review of
Literature,* LI (February 24, 1968). Also insightful, in part because it was
written by a highly promising younger black leader, is a review of *The
Souls of Black Folk,* by Joseph Rhodes, Jr., "Reconsideration: W.E.B.
Du Bois," *New Republic,* CLXVI (February 26, 1972).

Contemporaries and scholars have also examined separate facets of
Du Bois' multifaceted career. For Du Bois the sociologist, for example,
see E. Digby Baltzell, "Introduction to the 1967 Edition" of *The
Philadelphia Negro* . . . (1967). Some studies of Du Bois the historian
are: Herbert Aptheker, "Du Bois as Historian," *Negro History Bulletin,*
XXXII (April 1969); Jessie P. Guzman, "W.E.B. Du Bois—the Historian,"
Journal of Negro Education, XXX (Fall 1961); William Leo Hansberry,
"W.E.B. Du Bois' Influence on African History," *Freedomways,* V (Winter
1965); chapters in Earl E. Thorpe's historiographical studies, *The Central
Theme of Black History* (1969), and *Black Historians: A Critique* (1958,
1969); and Charles H. Wesley, "Du Bois the Historian," *Freedomways* V
(Winter 1965). Scholars have also studied Du Bois as a writer of fiction;
suggestive are Robert Bone, *The Negro Novel in America* (1958); and
David Littlejohn, *Black on White: A Critical Survey of Writing by Amer-*

ican Negroes (1966). The subject of Du Bois as Pan-Africanist has also stimulated the writing of several scholarly articles; see, for example, Harold R. Isaacs' "Du Bois and Africa," *Race,* II (November 1960), and three articles by Clarence G. Contee (two in the *Journal of Negro History,* LIV and LVII [January 1969; January 1972]; and one in *A Current Bibliography of African Affairs,* II [February 1970]). In numerous passages in *The Crisis of the Negro Intellectual* (1967), Harold Cruse has investigated the intellectual aspects of Du Bois' endeavors; for if Du Bois was a propagandist, protest leader, and political radical, he was, above all, an intellectual. But most significant of all are the writings, most of them by black intellectuals, which assess the meaning of Du Bois' life and work in warmly personal terms. How, for example, did a reading of *The Souls of Black Folk* alter one's perspective on race in America? How did it feel to meet Du Bois for the first time—*the* W.E.B. Du Bois whose ideas were frequent topics of dinner-table conversation for countless black families, and whose writings in *The Crisis* were sources of validation for previously unarticulated feelings of anger and hope, bitterness and pride? Three of the best of these writings are Shirley Graham Du Bois' *His Day Is Marching On* . . . (1971); J. Saunders Redding, "Portrait . . . W.E. Burghardt Du Bois," *American Scholar,* XVIII (Winter 1948–49); and Henry Lee Moon's "Postcript: A Personal Note," in Moon's *The Emerging Thought of W.E.B. Du Bois* . . . (1972). Warm remembrances by a white friend are Herbert Aptheker's "To Dr. Du Bois—with Love" and "On the Passing of Du Bois," both in *Political Affairs,* XLII (February and October 1963).

Index